MEMORIES, DREAMS
AND
INNER VOICES

*

MICHAEL RUBY

Station Hill
of Barrytown

Published by Station Hill Press, Inc., 124 Station Hill Road, Barrytown, NY 12507, as a project of The Institute for Publishing Arts, Inc., in Barrytown, NY, a not-for-profit, tax-exempt organization [501(c)(3)], supported in part by grants from the New York State Council on the Arts, a state agency.

Online catalogue: www.stationhill.org
e-mail: publishers@stationhill.org

Design by Sherry Williams, Oxygen Design Group
Cover and interior photos courtesy of Michael Ruby

Fleeting Memories first appeared as an ebook, with photographs, from Ugly Duckling Presse; and *Inner Voices Heard Before Sleep* as an ebook from Argotist Ebooks. Some sections of *Dreams of the 1990s* and *Inner Voices Heard Before Sleep* first appeared in *Aught, Café Irreal, Castagraf* and *Ep;phany*.

The author would like to thank Garth Graeper of Ugly Duckling Presse; Jeffrey Side of Argotist Ebooks; and the following journal editors: Ron Henry, Laura Solomon, Alice Whittenburg, G.S. Evans and Jeffrey Gustavson.

The author also would like to thank some friends for their advice: Sam Truitt, Nancy Graham, Peter Baker and Jon Fried.

Library of Congress Cataloging-in-Publication Data

Ruby, Michael (Michael Handler)
Memories, dreams and inner voices / Michael Ruby.
    p. cm.
ISBN 978-1-58177-125-1 (alk. paper)
I. Title.
PS3618.U325M46 2012
811'.6--dc23
                    2012004805

CONTENTS

FLEETING MEMORIES

T HIS IS A COLLECTION OF MEMORIES that popped into my mind over a period of seven years at work, as a copy editor at *The Wall Street Journal*, across the street from the World Trade Center. As far as I can tell, the memories came from nowhere, with no relation to the mostly political articles I was editing about the Republican takeover of Congress, the government shutdown, Monica Lewinsky, the Starr Report, the downfall of Newt Gingrich, impeachment, Florida or *Bush v. Gore*. Many of the memories are glimpses of places, a street corner and nothing more, as if a major function of the mind were this continuous global positioning, this continuous murmuring, "Right now, I'm at the southeast corner of 10th Ave. and 64th St." The places are distributed fairly evenly over the course of my life, with a somewhat disturbing precedence given to the streets around my childhood home at 251 Montrose Ave. in South Orange, N.J.

I first became aware of these memories in my twenties, but it wasn't until my mid-thirties that I really paid attention to them. A cascade began when I learned that my wife, Louisa, was pregnant with our first child, Charlotte, in 1993. A few years later, when I was taking care of identical-twin babies, Emily and Natalie, as many as three memories would pop into my mind while I was changing a single diaper. I tended to view them as memories being killed off by the brain. This was the last time they would enter my consciousness—at least until I short-circuited the dynamic. Maybe so many memories popped up because a powerful new experience was killing out an old experience, taking over its "engram," or whatever. I didn't have a chance to write down many memories, which are truly fleeting, during child care. Almost all the memories in this book were written in the right-hand margin of a sheet I filled out every day at work with the names and headline sizes of the stories I handled. Usually, a memory or two a day would float up, sometimes more, sometimes none. The most that ever floated up was nine, I think. At the end of my shift, I would copy them into a little notebook, often to some raillery from Josh Rosenbaum, Peter Saenger or Tom Walker. I, of course, was happy to accomplish some psychic research at work. In later years, I would make a photocopy of the story sheet and add it to the pile in my desk drawer, turning in the original to the copy chief with the memories in the margin erased.

This steady drip of memories through the years, this slow accretion, began to dry up in the beginning of 2000. In the third week of the new millennium, I was loaned for a few months from the national news department to the foreign department, where they didn't fill out story sheets. When I returned to national news, we had finally shifted from our antiquated CSI computer system to a new one, Hermes, which enveloped much more of my mental space. I started recording memories again, but at a diminished rate. Instead of a couple a day, there was only one a week. That's where things stood on September 11th. Our building, the so-called World Financial Center 1, was severely damaged by the collapse of the south tower of the World Trade Center. The newspaper was dislocated to South Brunswick, N.J. I knew that years worth of memories, hundreds of copies of story sheets, were entombed in my desk. From the fragmentary reports available to us about the state of our offices, it sounded like my memories would be fine, a bit dusty at worst. I didn't care about them inordinately anyway, because my impulse had waned.

During that October, a few people were allowed to retrieve computer hard drives and the like from the WFC, but it was discouraged, and I figured I could wait until the dust settled. Then, we learned the copy desk was being permanently transferred to South Brunswick. Workmen were going to gather our belongings on the 9th floor of the WFC, take them to another floor, vacuum off any toxic dust, then box and ship them to South Brunswick. People who didn't know me would be handling my things—a recipe for disaster. The story sheets looked so unprepossessing someone could easily throw them out. Special dispensations were possible, but again discouraged. It took me about one second to decide to seek one. I walked over to the "wartime cubicle" of Cathy Panagoulias, my former boss, who was in charge of the move. "Cathy, you've got to save me. I've got the last part of a book manuscript in my middle desk drawer at 200 Liberty." "What is it?" "I know this might sound flaky, but you know the story sheets we fill out? Every day I wrote a couple of memories in the margins." Cathy rolled her eyes, but said OK. A few days later, I was notified that a special delivery of my things could be retrieved in the basement of Building 5 in the South Brunswick complex. The vast space was mostly empty, with a few small islands of boxes on the concrete floor, but I learned that in a month 15,000 boxes would be there. My unconscious out-of-order autobiography was safe, along with everything else, including the much-maligned pile of newspapers I always had on top of my desk. I was pleased in a way to find that my last memory was from September 10th, and that it was portentous. If our building had been destroyed by the attack, as one might have reasonably expected, all the memories after number 1035 would have been lost.

1. Steve Kurens' backyard in South Orange during childhood
2. Driving north on Ridgewood Rd. toward Montrose Ave. in South Orange
3. The face of one of the Kendig brothers at Camp Kennebec senior in Maine in the early 1970s
4. Birdshit-stained rocks in the strait between Ellis and McGrath ponds at Kennebec junior
5. The shady streets around the Schwabachers' house on the South Orange-Orange border
6. Driving west on Interstate 280 past Newark in the '80s
7. The woods below my grandparent's country house near Tanglewood during early childhood
8. The incredibly dark arms of Ned Patz at Kennebec senior
9. Indoor tennis tryouts against Larry Cobeen in 7th grade in the fall of '69
10. My brother Steve's room in back of an exterminator's shop in East Orange in the early '80s
11. Our boarder, Kelly Doerr, on the steps to the third floor during high school
12. A weedlot near Chicago's Union Station during a visit to my sister Liz in the late '80s
13. Drinking a Sprite and waiting for Dad at the Sunoco station after a Columbia High School tennis practice
14. Walking on South Orange Ave. near Joe Zente's house in 5th grade
15. Vose Ave. by the Mountain Station parking lot
16. Hanging out with Julian Hopkins on a lawn above Ridgewood Rd. in 8th grade
17. An Italian restaurant near Main St. in Orange during high school
18. Walking west up Irving Ave. to Charlton Ave.
19. Hiking up Winter Hill in Somerville, Mass., where I lived on and off from '78 to '81
20. Ralston Ave. by the Woldin and Howard houses
21. The dirt playground under the oaks near the kindergarten entrance to Marshall School
22. The brook behind the first-base line of the Little League majors diamond
23. Running into "Loony" and Ed Ublower at Herman's Sporting Goods on Route 22 during high school

24. Playing first doubles against Newark Academy in Livingston in 12th grade

25. Running into an ill Mike Barber during junior year at Harvard, the last time I saw my Kennebec and college friend

26. Dave Gurien's house on Summit Ave. in Maplewood during high school

27. Steve Kurens' big side yard on a quiet street

28. Driving south on shady Wyoming Ave. in Maplewood

29. Looking across Wyoming Ave. at the gates to Blanchard Rd. during junior high

30. Walking past the demolished high school on Broadway in Cambridge

31. Steve Kurens' backyard

32. Neal Besser's birthday party at South Mountain Reservation ("the Res") in 3rd grade

33. Visiting Oleh Matiash's house in Irvington with the Guriens during high school

34. Walking with Bea Bindman in the deep shade on Walton Ave. in Maplewood in 11th grade

35. Mac Gander's house in Green River, Vt., in the years after college graduation

36. Talking with Ellen Adler at South Mountain School playground after college graduation

37. Walking home elated from Cheryl Dunsker's house in Maplewood in 7th grade

38. Memorial Park in Maplewood

39. The tall rhododendron bushes outside the 4th grade entrance to Marshall School

40. Driving west on Route 10 to Stonybrook Day Camp

41. Driving through Richmond, Vt., to Lucy and Knox Cummin's house around '90

42. The squat concrete-and-pipe fence around the four Little League fields

43. Walking home on Valley St. from Columbia High

44. Andrea Mentzel's living room on the night she had second thoughts about me in 9th grade

45. Peter Goldman's house on top of the hill in Newstead during high school

46. The soccer fields below the outdoor bus station in Perugia during my year

abroad in '80

47. The corner of Museum St. and Beacon St. near my apartment in Somerville

48. The gelato store near Hotel Piccolo in Perugia

49. Patches of snow in the parking lot of the bowling alley near Eagle Rock in 7th grade

50. A blackhaw flowering in the field behind Owen Andrews' house in Alberene, Va., in '88

51. Steve Sinoway's house on Montrose Ave.

52. Driving on Prospect Ave. to the E.J. Korvette department store near Eagle Rock

53. Walking past the Famous Deli in South Orange Village in the '80s

54. Walking past the apartment building next to South Orange Junior High

55. Steve Kurens' backyard

56. Walking on Hartford Rd. to Centre St.

57. South Mountain Arena on Northfield Ave. in West Orange

58. Hanging out behind the memorial rock at the duck pond by SOJH

59. Cheselyn Amato's family's cottage at Beach Haven in the summer after high-school graduation

60. Rick Kaplin boiling water in no time during the "obstacle race" at Kennebec senior

61. Stumbling on Stonybrook Day Camp during a drive with Cynthia Zarin in western Jersey in '82

62. The basketball court at Marshall School

63. The bald spot where the batter stood in baseball games at our house on Montrose Ave.

64. Our muddy backyard on the dreary Saturday after Thanksgiving in 9th grade

65. The tennis courts at the South Orange community center

66. The red clay basketball court at Kennebec senior

67. Eating a lunch of cheese, green apples and milk in my room on Via G. Mameli in Perugia

68. A group camping trip in Stokes State Forest in western Jersey in 9th grade

69. The corner of Ridgewood Rd. and Montrose Ave.

70. The hall to the master bedroom at Grandma Gert's apartment on West 57th St. in Manhattan during childhood

71. The soccer field at Orange Park

72. Sitting with Louisa at the big park in Parma during our honeymoon in Northern Italy in '91

73. Wandering around Newstead with Mark Woldin looking for Andy Schiller's house in 8th grade

74. Visiting my high-school Latin teacher, Mrs. Wolf, at her garden apartment near Mountain Station

75. Walking with Kate Brunet up Lexington Ave. to a Tex-Mex place in the early '90s

76. Steve Kurens' kitchen

77. Sitting with Bea Bindman outside the gym entrance on a fateful day at the start of 12th grade

78. Dinner with Louisa at a seedy but good place in Genova during our honeymoon

79. Playing stickball at Marshall School

80. Driving outside Warsaw with Louisa's friend "Magic" during our big European trip in the fall of '92

81. Smoking outside the Metropolitan Opera in the early '90s

82. The basketball court on Broadway in Somerville where Mac Gander chipped my teeth in '81

83. Walking steeply downhill to the mensa after watching a sunset in Perugia

84. Visiting Anne Montgomery at her office at Harvard's Lowell House

85. A church near my apartment at 493 12th St. in Brooklyn, where I lived from '84 to '88

86. Steve Kurens' basement

87. Climbing a mountain in New Hampshire with "Uncle Si" Dunklee during trip season at Kennebec senior

88. Walking down a steep street to Rob and Kiwi's apartment in Perugia

89. Hitching with George Kane in the Sierras during a cross-country trip after I got my M.A. from Brown in '83

90. The shady basketball court on Beacon St. where I played against Mac Gander in '78

91. North Terminal at Newark Airport during the era of cheap fares in the early '80s

92. Buying big bags of potting soil at Pierson's Mill in Maplewood during high school

93. The sidewalk below Steve Weis's house on Beech Spring Rd. in South Orange

94. Driving down Laurel Canyon Blvd. toward Sunset Blvd. during a visit to my sister Alice in Los Angeles in the '70s

95. The pond at the 11th tee at Mountain Ridge Country Club ("the Club") during a college vacation

96. The Ultimate Frisbee parking lot near Columbia High

97. Struggling to build a fire in high winds with Neal Besser at Stokes Stakes Forest in 9th grade

98. The memorial rock at the duck pond by SOJH

99. The blacktop at Marshall School

100. Going to Bellin's on South Orange Ave. to pick up clothes for Kennebec junior

101. Walking toward the amusement park in Scheverningen during our big European trip

102. Walking with Cynthia Zarin on the Brooklyn Heights promenade during a graduate-school vacation

103. The night I did eight hits of acid at Jeff Pownes' house in 8th grade

104. A view of Frenchman Bay from Route 1 in Maine in the early '90s

105. The curving panoramic road above the university in Perugia

106. Looking north along the train tracks from South Orange station

107. Tommy Kalb's house on Wyoming Ave. in 7th grade

108. Riding bikes to Andy Freundlich's grandmother's apartment in Orange in 6th grade

109. Anne Doyle's parents' house in Hingham, Mass., on the day she married George Kane in '89

110. The dirt road downhill through the woods to the laurel grove at the Res

111. Watching the pier burn at the Canadian port of St. Andrews a few months ago, in August '94

112. Irvington bus terminal during junior high

113. The sharp turn on Via G. Mameli in Perugia

114. The famous time my brother Steve and Scott Starr tortured me with cigarettes at home in 5th grade

115. My green tent flap on a camping trip with the Guriens at Bear Mountain during high school

116. Walking along a big curve in the Seine during a visit to Kate Brunet early this year, in February '94

117. Watching a tennis match at Millburn High

118. The corner of Holland Rd. and South Orange Ave.

119. Canoeing in Vermont with Lucy and Knox Cummin

120. Harvesting a "pot field" with Mark Woldin on Vose Ave. in 9th grade

121. An all-day Boy Scout sled race in the snow near South Mountain Arena in 7th grade

122. Buying a piping-hot bagel with Owen Andrews in the meatpacking district during my New York walks in the early '90s

123. Sara Schechner's original house on Hamilton Rd. in 4th grade

124. Playing tennis with Peter Brodie at Seton Hall University during junior high

125. The obscure streets below Ridgewood Rd. near Flood's Hill

126. Phil Carson's house in Maplewood during high school

127. Jamie Siegel's house on a narrow Maplewood street in 11th grade

128. Cheryl Dunsker's original house in Maplewood in 7th grade

129. Wandering around the Seton Hall parking lot doing mischief in 6th grade

130. A chaotic hike at night in the woods near Sunfish Pond in western Jersey in 9th grade

131. Walking uphill to Dr. Straussberg's dentist office in South Orange on a late fall day

132. The tall rhododendrons outside the 4th grade entrance to Marshall School

133. Anne Reitman's apartment on Sacramento St. in Cambridge

134. Sitting with Jimmy Straus near Dana Alexander and Sue Dunklee in back of Watson Hall at Kennebec senior

135. Mrs. Wolf's apartment near Mountain Station

136. Finding a tall pot plant with Dave Turkel in a ditch near Pathmark on Valley St. in 12th grade

137. Running up the endless last escalator at Port Authority to catch the 107 bus to South Orange

138. Standing on the sidewalk between our house and the Brodie house

139. Walking alongside a hedge to class at Domaine Université in Grenoble during my year abroad

140. Riding up the escalator at the Pompidou Center during the visit to Kate Brunet

141. The U-Haul place in Union Square in Somerville the day before I moved to Providence in '81

142. Parker Ave. in front of Columbia High

143. Picking up Tommy Lehman in West Orange on the way to indoor tennis in 11th grade

144. Waiting at the stoplight at South Orange Ave. and Old Short Hills Rd. on the way to B'nai Jeshurun or Don's Drive-In or St. Barnabas Hospital

145. The block on Kingman Rd. where Matt Kassin and Ronnie Lombardi lived

146. The leafy road to Washington Rock in the Res

147. Throwing snowballs at cars on South Orange Ave. and Holland Rd. in 5th grade

148. The indoor tennis place on Pleasant Valley Way in West Orange

149. The Van Gogh Museum in Amsterdam during our big European trip

150. Steve Kurens' fixed-up basement in 7th grade

151. A street in Chinatown during my New York walks

152. Walking around Jim Joyner's deteriorating house during a visit to Owen Andrews in Alberene

153. Mitchell Price's front door in Maplewood during high school

154. Paul Gross's house in West Orange during junior high

155. Hitching with Neal Besser from Cranford back to South Orange in 9th grade

156. The ballfields at Marshall School

157. The duck pond by SOJH

158. The small green across the street from Eliot House at Harvard

159. The obscure street behind Steve Longo's house on Turrell Ave.

160. Sailing with Steve Riegel on an artificial lake in western Jersey during a college summer vacation

161. The candy store at the little business district on Ridgewood Rd. in Maplewood

162. Driving to Upsala College in East Orange to see a rock concert during junior high

163. The RISD coffeeshop on Benefit St. in Providence during graduate school

164. Walking with Mark Woldin past the town pool during a visit back to South Orange in the '90s

165. My brother David, a few months before his death on November 18, 1972, giving our brother Steve a ride to Prospect House in East Orange

166. Driving to a jazz club near Route 46 with Mark Woldin, Steve Riegel and Michael Kaplan during a college summer vacation

167. The brook between the old Board of Education building and new South Orange police station

168. Shakespeare class with Professor Gwynne Evans during junior year

169. The duck pond by SOJH

170. Driving with Bill Elson to Oklahoma oilfields during my cross-country trip

171. Ringing the bell at a decrepit palace with Bril frescoes in Rome during our big European trip

172. Union Square during a visit back to Somerville a few months ago, in September '94

173. Driving east under a tangle of roads to the Holland Tunnel in the '80s

174. Laurel Canyon Blvd. during a visit to L.A. in the '70s

175. Driving with Gary Lovesky on Alewife Brook Parkway in Cambridge in the fall after graduate school

176. Penn Station Newark during a college summer vacation

177. The Quicks' huge house on Montrose Ave. during junior high

178. Driving with Cynthia Zarin to her family's house on Shadow Lane in Great Neck in '81

179. Playing tennis against Matt Waldor in high school

180. Cliff Greenberg's house on Hartford Rd.

181. Walking with Ronnie Lombardi on Turrell Ave. toward South Orange Ave.

182. The shady space between the South Orange Public Library and the Board of Education

183. "Camping" with Patty Lafferty in Moira McGuire's backyard in West Orange in 9th grade

184. Walking with Nancy Hurrelbrinck on the boardwalk in Ocean Grove, N.J., a month after Dad's death on April 26, 1986

185. Stanley Rd. near Gene McLaughlin's house

186. Waiting for Louisa and Betsy McLearn in Sloane Square during our trip to London early this year, in February '94

187. Dining with Julia Klein at Toon's Thai restaurant in the West Village in '85

188. Passing Richard Rosenbaum's house on Charlton Ave.

189. Bea Bindman's house in Maplewood in the summer after high-school graduation

190. Driving south past the lit ballfield on Valley St. in Orange during a college summer vacation

191. Jefferson School in Maplewood during high school

192. Parking with Louisa in front of a nice frame house in Rockport, Mass., on that fatal day, April 26, 1986

193. Drinking coffee at a bar before visiting Siracusa's amphitheater during my trip to Sicily in '89

194. Cousin Sophie Hardt's apartment in Grandma Gert's building during childhood

195. Playing tennis on the courts by the South Orange pool in 9th grade

196. A street in Perugia during our big European trip

197. Trapped with Louisa in the locked Belvedere in Florence during our big European trip

198. Franklin St. in Tribeca during my New York walks

199. The smiling face of Mrs. Curtin, my SOJH social studies teacher

200. Walking with my Italian roommate Gino under the long colonnade in Foligno during my year abroad

201. The hedge topped by spiderwebs at Domaine Université in Grenoble

202. Uncle George Travis at a parking lot in Westwood the day after the Northridge earthquake

203. Sitting in Steve Kurens' TV room with the flagstone floor after college graduation

204. A steep street in Perugia

205. The South Orange community center

206. A café near the Eiffel Tower during our big European trip

207. Sitting on the grass under the big sycamores by the South Orange tennis courts

208. My sister-in-law Maude Kent's garage on Philadelphia's Main Line in the early '90s

209. Walking home over the Brooklyn Bridge with Ezra Palmer from *The Wall Street Journal* in '89

210. Abby Weinberg's house on Montrose Ave. in the fall after college graduation

211. Walking over the bridge across the Huntington River near Lucy and Knox Cummin's house

212. Norma Ziegler's mother's apartment on Valley St. in Maplewood in 12th grade

213. Walking back to Santa Croce through the 19th century section of Florence during our big European trip

214. Driving east past Shinnecock Hills golf club in Southampton anytime after the summer of '82

215. Riding home in the van from a CHS tennis match in Summit

216. Tim Neumann's house on Ralston Ave. in 7th grade

217. Route 17 near Tuxedo Park, N.Y., during a college vacation

218. Waiting for Dad to pick me up at the Sunoco station after CHS tennis practice

219. Walking back to the Blue Line from East Boston High School, where I was a substitute teacher in '81

220. An Our House meeting at Paul Werbin's house on Blanchard Rd. in 10th grade

221. Looking at the massif across the vale of Chamonix from Mt. Blanc during my year abroad

222. Cary Welch's apartment building on Sparks St. during a visit back to Cambridge in the '90s

223. Watching "Love American Style" at home during junior high

224. Indoor tennis on Pleasant Valley Way in West Orange during junior high

225. Waiting for Dad to pick me up at Dave Gurien's house in Maplewood during junior high

226. Handing in Little League uniforms at the end of the season in 5th grade

227. Taking the train back to New York from the printing plant in Bethpage during my time at *The Wall Street Transcript* in '84-'85

228. Stopping at a pizzeria with Louisa and the baby Charlotte in Staten Island in '94

229. Reading Charlotte Perkins Gilman's "The Yellow Wallpaper" in '90

230. Our next-door neighbor's house on Hartford Rd.

231. Taking the train back to New York from Bethpage

232. The corn plot near the tennis courts at Domaine Université in Grenoble

233. The dark gray streets of downtown Chicago during a visit to my sister Liz

234. Walking up that curving panoramic road to a pizzeria with good capricciosa in Perugia

235. The waterfront in Aberystwyth, Wales, during my trip to Britain in the fall of '90

236. Walking into E.J. Korvette on the day of Uncle Harry Wolf's funeral in '75

237. East Cedar Lane in Maplewood, where Dave Gurien, Mark Woldin and I got busted in 9th grade

238. Walking with Knox Cummin from Socrates sculpture park to the subway in Queens in '88

239. The apartment building next to SOJH where my 9th grade English teacher, Miss Ladd, lived

240. Driving up South Orange Ave. past Old Short Hills Rd. toward B'nai Jeshurun

241. Walking on a snowy road with Chuck Schwartz in Williamsville, Vt., during junior year

242. Driving on the old route to the Club during childhood

243. Driving west over iron bridges near Jersey City on the way to I-280 in the '80s or '90s

244. A street near my Grodzin great-grandparents' house in Connellsville, Pa., in '88

245. The old B'nai Jeshurun Sunday school on Montrose Ave.

246. The playground under the oaks at Marshall School

247. Dropping off Richard Breeden in Brooklyn Heights during a van ride home from the *Journal* in the late '80s

248. Steve Bauer's house on Irving Ave. during high school

249. Walking in the hall toward Grandma Gert's bedroom

250. Sitting on the steps of Bellin's clothing store in South Orange Village late at night in 8th grade

251. Walking with Owen Andrews to the supermarket in East Cambridge in '94

252. Driving home from Newark Airport with Dad during college or graduate school

253. The basketball court in Somerville where Mac Gander chipped my teeth in '81

254. The crowded campsite where Cynthia Zarin and I pitched our tent in Annecy during my year abroad

255. The A&P parking lot in East Hampton

256. The split-rail fence at the Club where they set up a merry-go-round every Memorial Day

257. The book aisles on the top floor of the Harvard Coop annex

258. Sitting on the porch of Alan Roberts' house in 8th grade

259. Visiting William Carlos Williams sites in Paterson with Peter Baker during graduate school

260. Learning to pole a canoe with Artie Clark at Kennebec senior

261. Pam Ehrenkranz in army pants at Paul Werbin's house in 9th grade

262. Pitching for Kennebec senior against Jimmy Grodnick at Camp Takajo

263. The spiral staircase in the Bessers' house in Vermont during junior high

264. Driving past the VA hospital and Glover's gas station in East Orange on the way to New York

265. Our family's hairpin shortcut to enter the Garden State Parkway in East Orange

266. The little crabapple tree across from Dad's apartment at 18 Prospect St.

during the last years of his life

267. A street in Perugia

268. Warwick Ave. near the Kaufmans' house

269. The parking lot of a shopping center on Bloomfield Ave. near the Club

270. Looking at blue flowers with Cynthia Zarin in front of Jane Shore's old house in Cambridge

271. Walking with Chris Murtagh around Seton Hall on the first anniversary of Dad's death

272. Walking up a steep street near Mutt & Jeff's sandwich shop on a visit back to Providence in '91

273. The hardware store in Union Square in Somerville during junior year

274. Walking around Battery Park during my lunch break at the *Transcript*

275. The mud room at the Bessers' house during junior high

276. Lowell House dining hall at Harvard

277. Driving with Gary Lovesky in Connecticut in the summer after sophomore year

278. Riding a bike on Soak Hides Rd. in East Hampton in the summer after graduate school

279. Getting off the Brooklyn-Queens Expressway at the Tillary St. exit in the '80s or '90s

280. CHS tennis practice at the South Orange community center

281. Driving in Vermont with Knox Cummin

282. Hanging out with Lavea Brachman at City Hall during my lunch break at the *Transcript*

283. Swimming at a quarry with Owen Andrews and two college girls, Stuart and Grace, in Virginia in '88

284. Crossing the Hudson River on the way to the Catskills during our driving tour of the Northeast in '94

285. The fire station near John and Mary Tittmann's house during a visit back to Cambridge

286. Playing a stock market game with my sister Liz in our second-floor hall during childhood

287. Driving past Glover's and the brick garden apartments on the way to the Garden State Parkway

288. Paul Werbin and Roree Iris making out at a party during junior high

289. The failed street mall in downtown Providence during graduate school

290. Driving past a failing drive-in theater on Route 10 near Whippany during childhood

291. Standing at the railing at Niagara Falls in the summer before 4th grade

292. Playing in Tim Neumann's yard on Ralston Ave. in 6th grade

293. Walking on the curving sidewalk on Grove Rd. across from Grove Park

294. Driving by Jackie Stevens' new and plusher house during high school

295. Looking for rides to New York on a Cornell bulletin board in the summer after college graduation

296. Walking along the highway near Dad's Tech Hifi store in East Brunswick in the summer after junior year

297. Mom and Dad staying at the Harvard Motor Inn during freshman year

298. The pond at Uncle Milton Handler's country house in Yorktown Heights, N.Y., during childhood

299. Walking up South Orange Ave. past the Famous Deli during junior high

300. Hiking with a German philosophy student named Helmut in a boulder field in the Alps near Grenoble

301. Walking through the Bio Labs on the way to my apartment at 119 Museum St. in Somerville

302. That all-day Boy Scout sled race in the snow

303. Walking past Andy Freundlich's old house to SOJH in 7th grade

304. Richard Solomon entering the Res near the Newstead watertower in 10th grade

305. Looking at the Kozaks' new house across Charlton Ave. in 6th grade

306. Visiting my brother Sandy and Ruth Richards in Milton, Mass., after the breakup with Cynthia Zarin in January '83

307. Walking home with John Conlon on Irving Ave. a week before high-school graduation

308. Walking with Esther Bromberg through Maplewood Village in 10th grade

309. Uncle Lou Sacks' house in Summit during the balmy Christmas before my year abroad

310. Walking up from the subway to Montague St. in Brooklyn Heights in the '80s or '90s

311. Handing in my Rotary Little League uniform at the end of the season in 7th grade

312. Driving on the Garden State Parkway to the apartment of my Tech Hifi boss, Lou Maresca, in Nutley

313. Walking with Cheselyn Amato on Vose Ave. in 12th grade

314. Crossing the bridge from the SOJH parking lot to the tennis courts

315. The vacant lot on Vose Ave. where I made out with Judy Levine in 9th grade and Cheselyn Amato in 12th grade

316. Walking to Steve Kurens' house for lunch on an early spring day in 4th grade

317. The basketball hoop in Neal Besser's driveway during junior high

318. The face of Charlie Cohen from Stonybrook Day Camp

319. Steve Weis's house on Beech Spring Rd.

320. Looking at the huge Kenneth Snelson sculpture at Storm King Arts Center in the late '80s

321. The A&P parking lot in East Hampton

322. Mitchell Price's house in Maplewood during high school

323. The parking lot at Pal's Cabin near Eagle Rock during the last years of Dad's life

324. Walking around leafy Durham during my trip to Britain

325. CHS tennis coach Vic Lomakin saying he wasn't going to play me because of my long hair

326. Taking mushrooms with George Kane in Desolation Wilderness during my cross-country trip

327. Stopping for ice cream at Welsh Farms near the Club

328. Bright sunlight in the Club parking lot

329. The face of *Journal* editor Ron Smith anytime from '86 until he died of AIDS in '94

330. The Howards' house on leafy Ralston Ave.

331. Looking over the railing at people down below in the old snackbar at the Club

332. A street in Chamonix

333. Andrea Mentzel's house in Maplewood that night in 9th grade

334. Driving north on Prospect Ave. past E.J. Korvette

335. The Howards' house on leafy Ralston Ave.

336. The face of Coach Jim Voltaggio of Rotary in 7th grade

337. Mama Rondolini's apartment, the first place I lived in Perugia

338. Driving on Route 18 to Dad's Tech Hifi store in New Brunswick during a college summer vacation

339. Walking up to a wild party at Jane Koenig's house on Memorial Day weekend in 8th grade

340. Eating with Mom and Dad at a quiche place on Boylston St. in Cambridge during senior year

341. "Uncle Ray" Dallaire at Kennebec junior

342. Cliff Greenberg's backyard on Hartford Rd.

343. The South Orange community house

344. Walking on shady Hartford Rd. toward Centre St.

345. Walking to class at Domaine Université in Grenoble

346. Looking at the train tracks from Valley St. on the Maplewood border

347. A rare time driving out to the printing plant in Bethpage

348. Driving along the west side of Seton Hall, where Dad rear-ended someone once

349. The stores built in '70 at the corner of South Orange Ave. and Scotland Rd. that never did well

350. The drive through Irvington to the Garden State Parkway on the way to Tech Hifi

351. Sitting in a lawn chair talking to Tory Garvin at the Latin Club picnic in 12th grade

352. Dave Gurien's father's apartment in Arlington, N.J., shortly after I moved to New York in October '83

353. The ill-starred Heather McClave's English 10 class in Eliot House basement during sophomore year

354. Playing near the Schechners' first house on Hamilton Rd. in 4th grade

355. Walking along the tall fence of the minor-league ballfield on the way to SOJH

356. That obscure street behind Steve Longo's house

357. Driving down Forest Rd. after indoor tennis in 7th grade

358. A misty night outside Maxwell's in Hoboken in '94

359. Drinking with Mark Woldin at Stuffed Shirt in the summer after high-school graduation

360. The face of David Joselit from Harvard

361. Getting my name stenciled in white thread on a blue cap at the '65 World's Fair in Queens

362. Waiting outside Dave Gurien's house in Maplewood

363. Listening to Otis Redding at Kate Brunet's apartment in Belleville earlier this year, in May '95

364. Mom backing out of Alex Tint's steep driveway in West Orange at the beginning of memory

365. Walking over the hill to Jimmy Gander's apartment on the Somerville-Malden border during senior year

366. Driving near the Davimos house on Gregory Ave. in West Orange

367. Seeing a patch of white clover from Deena Shoshkes and Jon Fried's car in East Hampton in '85

368. Tagging along with Saul Perl to the apartment of a hip Italian couple on my side of Perugia

369. The big tree on Parker Ave. across from Columbia High

370. The Dover stop where Dad caught the bus to work when he had car troubles in the early '70s

371. Picking an ear of corn in that little plot near the tennis courts in Grenoble

372. Driving on Ridgewood Rd. past Flood's Hill toward SOJH

373. Stopping near a smoke-belching Maine paper plant on an overnight drive with Owen Andrews from Nova Scotia to Vermont in August '85

374. The bottom of the hill by the Old Stone Bank in Providence during graduate school

375. Walking up the steps to the Res from Claremont Ave. in Maplewood during high school

376. Drinking Shirley Temples when they set up a bar by the Club pool on holiday weekends

377. The time Dave Turkel and I discovered the pot plant by Pathmark

378. Walking with Louisa to the stream behind my family's old house near Tanglewood on our first wedding anniversary in '90

379. Riding a bus to Chicago's O'Hare airport on a frigid and fateful day in December '88

380. Playing near Lisa Kaufman's house during childhood

381. The Haddads' street near Marshall School during high school

382. Taking a bus uphill past villas to the church overlooking Bologna during our honeymoon

383. The kindergarten entrance to Marshall School

384. Walking out to Jimmy Gander's apartment on the Somerville-Malden border

385. Buying Liubov Popova postcards at a shop in Soho in the mid-'80s

386. Driving from South Orange to the Garden State Parkway during childhood

387. The back entrance to the palace in Vienna during our big European trip

388. A piano lesson at Kenneth Amaro's house in Newstead in 1st grade

389. Passing the Pakonis house on Scotland Rd.

390. The candy store at the little business district on Ridgewood Rd. in Maplewood

391. Walking on 2nd Ave. during my first years in New York

392. The late sunlight on Irvington High during a drive home from Tech Hifi

393. Looking south down the train tracks from South Orange station

394. The basketball court on Beacon St. in Somerville where Mac Gander and I played

395. Sleighing at night with Dave Gurien on Flood's Hill during high school

396. Looking at the restored Sistine Chapel ceiling during our big European trip

397. Walking past the new AT&T building in Lower Manhattan during my New York walks

398. My brother David's friend John Cosman's house on Montrose Ave.

399. Walking along Ridgewood Rd. above the duck pond

400. Snowy streets near my brother Sandy's house in Milton

401. Playing first doubles against Newark Academy

402. Tagging along with Saul Perl to the apartment of the hip Italian couple

403. The gate to the park at the newly built American Academy in Cambridge

in '81

404. Sex on a mountainside with Cynthia Zarin near Aix-les-Bains during my year abroad

405. Trying to sneak into a rock concert at Upsala in East Orange during junior high

406. Talking with a retired phone operator in Manchester, Mass., a few days after our wedding on August 19, 1989

407. Driving away from the Maine paper plant that night with Owen Andrews

408. Jane Lowell's house on Irving Ave. in 10th grade

409. Walking down Dad's hallway from the elevator during the last years of his life

410. Walking at dusk near Mark Woldin's apartment on 30th St. in the early '90s

411. Driving down to Gregory Ave. from Prospect Ave. in West Orange

412. Waiting at the clammy back entrance of Widener Library during a visit to Harvard in '89

413. Standing at the split-rail fence along the 18th hole at the Club during childhood

414. The bar near the archaeological museum in Siracusa

415. Getting a ride with Jack Barnes back to New York from the printing plant in Bethpage

416. The South Orange tennis courts during high school

417. Walking with Dave Turkel to the Tufts computer center in the summer after 11th grade

418. Walking east on Nassau St. in Lower Manhattan during my time at the *Transcript*

419. Gary Lovesky's house on Cameron Ave. in Cambridge on a dreary day in the early '80s

420. Cruising around the town of Catskill during our driving tour of the Northeast

421. Summit Ave. near Dave Gurien's house in Maplewood

422. The sweeping curve on the canal in Leiden during our big European trip

423. Looking at the apple tree next door on Hartford Rd. in 7th grade

424. The outdoor terrace on top of the Pompidou Center during our big European trip

425. Crossing the bridge over the Huntington River near Lucy and Knox Cummin's house

426. Walking home from Columbia High on Valley St.

427. The face of Chuck Schwartz that time in Williamsville

428. Digging latrines with Boy Scouts in the sandy Pine Barrens in 6th grade

429. The motel in Harvard Square where Mom and Dad stayed during freshman parents' week

430. Watching Marilyn Monroe in "Niagara" at our apartment at 133 Garfield Pl. in '95

431. Dave Turkel outside Pathmark

432. Peter Baker pointing out April Bernard's old building near the Manhattan Bridge in the mid-'80s

433. The ill-starred Jonathan Grandine's class on the epic in Emerson Hall during sophomore year

434. Kathy Kennedy's house in West Orange sometime in the '70s

435. Picking up the U-Haul truck to move from Somerville to Providence

436. Walking with Louisa in the picnic field at the Res a year and a half after Dad died

437. Walking past the blue chalet in Winter Harbor, Maine, during our second summer there in '92

438. Attending a reading by Alice Lichtenstein under the Brooklyn Bridge in '90

439. Waiting for the train back to New York from Bethpage

440. Looking at the watertower near my father-in-law Bill Wood's farm in Pennsyvania in the early '90s

441. Driving on Route 128 to Louisa's family's summer house in Manchester anytime from '85 to '90

442. Walking through Brooklyn's Cobble Hill on New Year's Day of '91

443. Walking past the huge Helmsley building north of Manhattan's meatpacking district in the late '80s

444. Taking the spiral stairs up from the ping-pong room in the Bessers' house in Vermont in 10th grade

445. Driving past the old Danceteria in the Hamptons

446. Playing catch with Joe Zente in the melting snow in my next-door

neighbor's yard in 4th grade

447. Throwing snowballs outside the Eagle Rock bowling alley in 7th grade

448. Driving to Uncle Milton's summer house in Westhampton in the early '90s

449. Walking home from subbing in the Charlestown section of Boston

450. The Ivy Hill bus stop on Irvington Ave. during a college vacation

451. Walking up Winter Hill during my last year in Somerville

452. Driving to the old North Terminal of Newark Airport during high school

453. Entering the Long Island Expressway at Exit 70 on the drive home to Brooklyn from East Hampton

454. Taking the Red Line to Ashmont on a frigid day to visit my brother Sandy after his heart attack in '81

455. The doctor's office on South Orange Ave. near Joe Zente's house in 5th grade

456. Playing tennis with Steve Riegel in Maplewood during a college vacation

457. Going with Mark Woldin to watch the Super Bowl at Tim Neumann's apartment in Hoboken in '87

458. Driving past Nancy Enzminger's house in South Orange during high school

459. Waiting on the platform for the train at East Hampton station

460. Aunt Toni and Uncle Abe Chayes' house in Cambridge during high school or college

461. Walking from Dad's car to the Tech Hifi store in New Brunswick

462. An afternoon of vandalism at the kindergarten entrance to Marshall School after 6th grade graduation

463. Walking with Owen Andrews over the Pepperpot Bridge during a visit back to Cambridge

464. Driving my brother Steve to Prospect Ave. in East Orange during high school

465. Walking north on the Magnificent Mile in Chicago during my first visit to my sister Liz

466. The T. Wistar Brown house in Winter Harbor earlier this year, in August '95

467. Walking with Peter Baker along the Seekonk River during a visit back to

Providence in the late '80s

468. Stopping at the toll plaza after getting off the Jersey Turnpike in New Brunswick

469. Walking in a dry streambed near my sister Alice's house in Pacific Palisades at the end of graduate school

470. The section of Perugia near the bus station and small soccer stadium

471. Looking at a Victorian turret on Montrose Ave. near the old B'nai Jeshurun Sunday School during a visit back to South Orange

472. Walking through the big town parking lot in East Hampton at night

473. The skinny park on the bend in the East River at Houston St. during my New York walks

474. Snug Harbor arts center in Staten Island in '90

475. The cliff walk in Newport during graduate school

476. Returning from the Warsaw Ghetto on a frigid boulevard at night during our big European trip

477. Walking in the snowy Res with Ellen Hamingson and Sara Schechner during freshman year

478. Sleighing at Flood's Hill during childhood

479. Visiting my sophomore tutor Larry Hannawalt at his house in Cambridge after his breakdown

480. Walking toward the fieldstone pumphouse at Grove Park during a visit back to South Orange

481. The dinner with Louisa's siblings on the Main Line when we hid she was pregnant in '93

482. Passing Bellin's for Girls during junior high

483. Hitting tennis balls with Matt Waldor during junior high

484. Crossing Berkeley Ave. on the way to Steve Kurens' house for lunch in 4th grade

485. Running to Dad's car to escape from a group of New Brunswick muggers

486. Looking at houses out the window of a train to Philadelphia on Christmas Eve in the early '90s

487. Driving around New Brunswick to scope out a high-end competitor of Tech Hifi

488. Leafletting Rutgers' campus for Tech Hifi

489. The boat dock in back of Uncle Milton's house in Westhampton

490. Driving on Route 18 to the light where I always turned left into New Brunswick

491. Watching the pathetic deerhunting scene in "The Deer Hunter" at the Harvard science center

492. Seeing "Stranger Than Paradise" near Lincoln Center on my first date with Louisa in '85

493. Driving by Fred Hatt's place in Brooklyn's Greenpoint in '95

494. Exploring Brooklyn's Bay Ridge with Louisa during my New York walks

495. David Bromberg making a surprise appearance at a concert at Eagle Rock during high school

496. Paul Werbin and Roree Iris making out at a party during junior high

497. Andrea Mentzel's living room that night in 9th grade

498. Playing football outside in the cold during gym at SOJH

499. Playing the pinball machine in Dave Turkel's basement in 12th grade

500. Seeing my brother Steve's friend Don Schneier at a CHS soccer practice during Little League

501. Watching "Angel Heart" with Louisa at Garfield Pl.

502. Crossing a bridge on the way to Versailles during a visit to Kate Brunet in Paris

503. The big bend on Route 128 on the home stretch of the drive to Manchester

504. The South Orange community center's basketball courts during childhood

505. The Kentile building in Brooklyn's Gowanus on a dreary day during my New York walks

506. Driving south past E.J. Korvette in the deep shade of white pine trees

507. The night when Jimmy Gander and John Phillips yelled out the window at a parked van on Norfolk St. in Cambridge during junior year

508. Walking on Route 18 outside Tech Hifi in East Brunswick

509. Driving south on Wyoming Ave. toward South Orange Ave. during a visit back to South Orange

510. Taking a shortcut past the high school to East Hampton's Main Beach in the '90s

511. Walking by Rita Murray's old house on Warwick Ave. during a visit back to South Orange

512. Playing basketball in Steve Riegel's driveway in Maplewood in 12th grade

513. Driving past Irvington High on the way home from the Garden State Parkway

514. Driving with Bill Wood through the mill section of Ellsworth, Maine, in '94

515. Walking around the Roman Forum during our big European trip

516. Driving south on Clark St. toward Montrose Ave. during a visit back to South Orange

517. Going with Shael Brachman to our Ruby great-grandparents' house in Marietta, Ohio, in '92

518. The quadrangle at Columbia University during my New York walks

519. Reading Williams' Spring and All at Aunt Emily Wood's house in Bridgehampton in '92

520. Watching "Twin Peaks" on TV at Garfield Pl.

521. Watching the sunset on the pier in Bay Ridge during my New York walks

522. Sitting on Alan Roberts' porch after failing to get tickets to the "Grateful Dead" concert at the Fillmore East in 8th grade

523. Looking at the beautiful marble steps of the Providence library with Gary Lovesky during graduate school

524. Dinner with Mom and my stepfather, Eli Pearce, at Monastero in East Hampton in the early '90s

525. Eddie Verner's house on Stanley Rd. in South Orange

526. Walking with Neal Besser on a cold night to Barbara Wood's house in West Orange in 9th grade

527. That misty night outside Maxwell's in Hoboken

528. Going to the South Orange Public Library during junior high

529. Walking in a garden across the Cam from one of the Cambridge colleges during our '94 trip

530. Ronni Janoff's house in Maplewood during high school

531. A street in Bath during my trip to Britain

532. Entering the Garden State Parkway from downtown Irvington on the way to Tech Hifi

533. Getting off the LIE East at Exit 70 on the way to East Hampton

534. Seeing Larry Hannawalt on the street near Harvard

535. Passing the VA hospital on the way to the Garden State Parkway

536. Those red-brick houses near Matt Kassin's on Kingman Rd.

537. The '50s sci-fi movie about a woman who turns into a giant on "Chiller Theater" during childhood

538. Sitting on lush grass with Peter Baker near my old house on Montrose Ave. during graduate school

539. Stopping for drinks with Janet Murray at a jazz bar on Flatbush Ave. after seeing a dance at BAM in '91

540. Visiting Plum Island near Newburyport, Mass., a few days after our wedding

541. Looking for a new bed in the East 30s in Manhattan a few weeks after Dad died

542. The shady part of Hartford Rd. near the Reillys' house during early childhood

543. Looking at dead fish floating in the Providence River with Gary Lovesky during graduate school

544. Taking local roads during a trafficky Sunday night drive home from the Hamptons in the early '90s

545. The Howards' house on leafy Ralston Ave.

546. Looking at the starry sky with Deena Shoshkes and Cheryl Dunsker at Putney School in Vermont in the summer after 11th grade

547. Steve Kurens' basement in 7th grade

548. Canoeing on a lake near Lucy and Knox Cummin's house in Vermont

549. Meeting Julian Hopkins near the brook before the famous party at Jane Koenig's house in 8th grade

550. The face of Norma Ziegler from high school

551. That apple tree in the middle of the yard next door during childhood

552. The face of my brother David

553. The crappy lake at Aix le Bains during my year abroad

554. Hiding a plastic bag of pills in a hole near the Pioneer tennis courts at Kennebec senior

555. Seeing Jerome Hines sing at the Ray Sterling memorial concert in South

Orange in 6th grade

556. A nighttime visit to the White Castle in Orange during high school

557. The chilly Little League tryouts in 4th grade

558. An impromptu drive with Owen Andrews to his grandparents' old house in Barrie, Mass., in '93

559. The gardens at Tanglewood on our first wedding anniversary

560. Driving south from Connellsville after visiting my Grodzin great-grandparents' house

561. Stopping for gas at the end of that overnight drive to Vermont with Owen Andrews

562. Driving north on FDR Drive around 14th St. in Manhattan in the '90s

563. Driving down Route 114 to Route 27 in East Hampton

564. Walking up that curving panoramic road above the university in Perugia

565. Playing tennis with Steve Riegel in Maplewood during a college summer vacation

566. Riding home to Brooklyn from the *Journal* in Clive's van

567. Dropping Harris Collingwood and Emily Singer at the hotel on Route 128 before Gary Lovesky's wedding in '86

568. Walking through Union Square in Somerville during senior year

569. The lake at Uncle Milton's house in Yorktown Heights

570. Walking near Gary Lovesky's house on Cameron Ave.

571. The first glimpse of Peconic Bay off Sebonac Rd. during a drive to the Hamptons in the '90s

572. Owen Andrews asking me to be his best man at Mt. Auburn Cemetery in Cambridge in '91

573. Walking down to Ridgewood Rd. after getting ripped off at Donny Wachenfeld's house in 8th grade

574. The red-brick house at Ralston Ave. and Charlton Ave. during a visit back to South Orange

575. Watching a movie at Garfield Pl. about '50s teenagers in love at a family beach house

576. The Jordan St. Coop at Harvard during senior year

577. A blighted stretch of Delancey St. during my New York walks

578. Driving west on Central Ave. over the Garden State Parkway in East

Orange

579. The pool table in Steve Kurens' basement

580. Walking along the edge of the Little League field below the community house

581. Walking around Newstead during junior high

582. Looking across Montrose Ave. at the Giannotto house

583. The centro in Perugia

584. Driving down Northfield Ave. to Gregory Rd. in West Orange

585. The open doors of the houses in Newburyport a few days after our wedding

586. Sunfish Pond in 9th grade

587. Looking at the statue celebrating the invention of ether in Boston Common in '85

588. Hearing about the Shah's death with Cynthia Zarin in Annecy during my year abroad

589. The bus arriving at Kennebec junior at the beginning of summer

590. The pumping station in Grove Park during a visit back to South Orange

591. Knox Cummin picking up Louisa and me at Burlington airport

592. Gary Lovesky mentioning "slurry" while we waited for a bus at the end of graduate school

593. Stopping to look at a weedlot with Cynthia Zarin while apartment-hunting in Providence

594. Hemlock Falls at the Res

595. That big tree across the street from Columbia High

596. Taking the train to Chartres with Louisa and Kate Brunet

597. Driving with Sara Schechner and Gary Yellen to math teacher Halsey Stickel's house in Basking Ridge during freshman year

598. Picking corn that time near the tennis courts in Grenoble

599. The front of the South Orange Public Library

600. Calling home from a phone booth at Maplewood's Memorial Park after hanging out with Esther Bromberg in 10th grade

601. Driving with Bill Wood past white motel cottages near Ellsworth

602. Sue Straussberg's house on Hartford Ct. in South Orange

603. The face of Stu Richter, my 12th grade biology teacher

604. Playing basketball at Neal Besser's house during junior high

605. Driving on Storrow Drive toward East Cambridge in the mid-'90s

606. Hanging out with Sandy Stillman in Ithaca in the summer after college graduation

607. Leaving the Pathmark parking lot during a college vacation

608. The beginning of the drive with Harris Collingwood, Emily Singer and Owen Andrews to Gary Lovesky's wedding

609. Going out to dinner with Owen Andrews in the Mabou Highlands in Nova Scotia

610. Playing near Kevin Gilroy's house and the VA hospital in 6th grade

611. That day with Mike Barber near Inman Square in Cambridge

612. Driving Mom to her dentist in Livingston in the early '90s

613. Those spring days after school with Bea Bindman in 11th grade

614. Walking with Owen and Eleanor Andrews near my brother Sandy's house in Charlestown during a visit back to Cambridge

615. Waiting for a ride in the parking lot across the street from E.J. Korvette

616. Nearing the LIE on the drive home from East Hampton

617. The face of Rick Spiers from Harvard

618. The face of Lavea Brachman in the fall after graduate school

619. The section of Perugia where I first lived

620. A day at the Fellsway with Gary Lovesky in the fall after graduate school

621. Looking at a ritzy Brooklyn Heights house with Patrick Bunyan and Scott Byrne earlier this year, in March '96

622. That last stretch of Route 128 before Manchester

623. Seeing Ed and Ridgely Biddle's friend Simon at a restaurant in East Hampton in '94

624. The Sohiers' house in Manchester a few days before our wedding

625. Visiting a lake with Owen Andrews in Carlisle, Mass., a few days before his wedding

626. Driving through an evergreen forest in northwest Jersey during early childhood

627. The shady drive from Mylene Hodgson's house down to the beach in

Fairfield, Conn., in '84

628. Driving with Gary Lovesky on Alewife Brook in Cambridge

629. The big tree that overhangs the 18th hole at the Club during a college summer vacation

630. That shady playground under the oaks at Marshall School during a visit back to South Orange

631. Walking on Warwick Ave. near the Schwabachers' house

632. The face of Anne Montgomery, my Bible teacher at Harvard

633. Stopping for gas near the Mass Pike after a dinner at Gary Lovesky's house in Wayland in the early '90s

634. Stopping to get Owen Andrews' car fixed on our first day in Nova Scotia

635. Driving north along Lake Michigan and stopping at a park during a visit to my sister Liz in Chicago

636. The time the cops caught us throwing snowballs at cars from inside the fence of the VA hospital, and Kevin Gilroy almost got away, but Joe Zente told on him

637. A late-night powwow with Matt Waldor and other former CHS superstars in the Stillmans' backyard after college graduation

638. Driving past the octagonal church in Richmond, Vt., near Lucy and Knox Cummin's house

639. Watching the great Steve Kendall of Millburn High cream CHS's Billy Kragen in tennis

640. Eddie Verner's red-brick front steps in 5th grade

641. Hanging out with Pam Ehrenkranz and Jesse Ribot outside that candy store on Ridgewood Rd. during high school

642. Reading Marcel Proust in the car outside Tech Hifi in East Brunswick

643. Walking with Bea Bindman through Memorial Park on the day she sprung the word "platonic" on me

644. A street in Lubec, Maine, in the early '90s

645. Watching David Bromberg play at Eagle Rock on a June night during high school

646. The farm country where the St. John River joins the Allagash during trip season at Kennebec senior

647. Looking down at the Yellowstone River gorge with my sister Alice and

Dad in '82

648. Walking around Greenwich on a snowy morning during our trip to London

649. A boat trip with Uncle Milton and Aunt Miriam near Moriches Inlet in '91

650. Stopping for lunch in the cemetery in Pottsville, Pa., during our driving tour of the Northeast

651. Sizing up the golf course in Sorrento, Maine, with Maude and Tim Kent

652. The face of Larry Hannawalt from Harvard

653. The face of lifelong family friend Michael Stern

654. A party at Peter Goldman's house in Newstead during high school

655. Laurie Manelli's place in Brooklyn's Carroll Gardens in the mid-'80s

656. Harbor Hill, a beautiful house in Winter Harbor

657. Visiting Julia Klein in Philadelphia in '85

658. The Irvington bus terminal during high school

659. Playing Twister at Roree Iris's house in 8th grade

660. Buying books for class on the top floor of the Harvard Coop annex

661. Those obscure streets near Flood's Hill

662. The supermarket parking lot near Lili Porten and Jim Gussen's apartment during a visit back to Cambridge

663. Driving past the golf course on Pleasant Valley Way in Verona on the way to the Club

664. That white mansion at Montrose Ave. and Ridgewood Rd. that sold for $125,000 in the early '70s

665. Picking up my sister Liz at Little Cottage nursery school

666. The newsstand at South Orange station during the last years of Dad's life

667. Driving out of Livingston Mall onto Eisenhower Parkway during a college summer vacation

668. That walk with Owen and Eleanor Andrews to Charlestown

669. The time Keith Roberts defended Mark Woldin and hit me in the head with an iceball outside Eddie Verner's house in 6th grade

670. Harry (now Strauss) Zelnick's house on Mayhew Dr. during junior high

671. That time my brother David drove our brother Steve to Prospect House

672. Playing 3rd singles rather poorly for CHS against East Orange in 12th grade

673. Playing tennis on the lower courts at Memorial Park during a college summer vacation

674. Brilliant wildflowers at the back of the amphitheater in Siracusa

675. The row of trees at Marshall School planted in honor of dead and retired teachers

676. Playing tennis badly against Matt Waldor during high school

677. Stopping for gas at the end of that overnight drive to Vermont with Owen Andrews

678. Playing Ultimate Frisbee in the CHS parking lot during a college vacation

679. Tim Healy's house on Charlton Ave.

680. The private road near my house on Montrose Ave.

681. Leafletting for Tech Hifi

682. Reading John Updike's Rabbit, Run at home with pneumonia on Garfield Pl. in October '93

683. Driving north with Gary Lovesky toward Alewife Brook in Cambridge

684. The corner of Ralston Ave. and Charlton Ave. during a visit back to South Orange

685. Standing outside the somewhat Stalinist Omaha museum during a visit to my sister Liz in '93

686. Walking by Cathy Goodwin's house on Grove Rd. on a green, green day in 6th grade

687. Playing stickball with Carl Adamo on the blacktop at Marshall School in 7th grade

688. Driving with Dad over the bridge from Harrison to Newark to catch a train to Tech Hifi

689. Handing in Little League uniforms at the end of a season

690. Walking with Peter Baker along the Seekonk River to the big cemetery in Providence

691. Leafletting Rutgers dorms for Tech Hifi

692. Walking around the duck pond by SOJH

693. Mark Woldin's house on Ralston Ave.

694. Walking on one of the West Side piers near Christopher St. in the late '80s

695. Visiting Lavea Brachman at Harvard's Lowell House in the fall after graduate school

696. Bumming money from an older girl named Sandra at her house in Maplewood in 8th grade

697. Talking with Knox Cummin about the size of the universe while walking up 3rd Ave. one morning in '90

698. Stopping for a burger with Owen Andrews in deserted Staunton, Va., on a Sunday afternoon in the late '80s

699. Dave Turkel's MIT frat house in Boston during freshman year

700. Looking at the Peruzzi frescoes in the Farnesina in Rome during our big European trip

701. Talking to Bob Brennan on the van ride home from the *Journal*

702. A bookstore at MIT during college

703. Stopping to look at that weedlot with Cynthia Zarin in Providence

704. Driving around the big bend on Gregory Ave. near Kathy Kennedy's house in West Orange

705. Leafing through a math textbook at MIT that cited my brother Sandy's '60s research

706. Walking past Richard Rosenthal's house on Woodland Pl. during junior high

707. A wacky drive to Owen and Eleanor Andrews' rehearsal dinner in Boston

708. A Latin Club party at Mrs. Wolf's apartment

709. Reading the Newark library section of Philip Roth's Goodbye, Columbus at Garfield Pl. in '95

710. The British-born, black copy editor named Joseph who briefly worked at the *Journal*

711. Walking with Louisa and Kate Brunet to Musée Marmattan in Paris

712. The little court on Beacon St. in Somerville where Mac Gander and I played basketball

713. The bulletin board at an American student hangout in Prague during our big European trip

714. Driving to Alex Tint's birthday party in West Orange in the summer before kindergarten

715. The prison near the church compound in Durham during my trip to

Britain

716. Dave Gurien's father's apartment in Arlington

717. The bend on Grove Rd. in front of Marshall School during a visit back to South Orange

718. Driving back to New York in heavy traffic from the printing plant in Bethpage

719. Crossing the footbridge over the brook to the dusty SOJH tennis courts

720. Looking closely at the old red-brick building on 3rd St. and 3rd Ave. in Brooklyn with Knox Cummin during my New York walks

721. Crossing a scary street by the waterfront in Gloucester on that fatal day, April 26, 1986

722. Playing paddle tennis with Cheselyn Amato in 12th grade

723. Hurrying from the parking garage to Owen and Eleanor Andrews' rehearsal dinner

724. Eating quiche with a divorced Mom and Dad on Boylston St. in Cambridge during senior year

725. That day with Peter Baker at the falls in Paterson

726. The cul de sac on Woodland Crescent near our house on Montrose Ave.

727. Finding the pot plant with Dave Turkel near Pathmark

728. Throwing snowballs at cars on South Orange Ave. by that doctor's office near Joe Zente's house

729. Stu Richter giving me cactus and succulent cuttings at his house in Maplewood in 10th grade

730. Reading William Kennedy's <u>Billy Phelan's Greatest Game</u> on the subway to work in early '94

731. Picking up our dog Sheik at Buddy Cohen's farm in western Jersey in the summer before 5th grade

732. Bloomfield Park in the '70s

733. Driving with Dad to Herman's to buy camping equipment in 10th grade

734. Looking at I-280 from the dead end on Babcock Pl. in West Orange, where my brother Steve lived in the '80s and early '90s

735. A beautiful street in Brooklyn's Carroll Gardens during my New York walks

736. Buying a gas cooking stove at the hypermarket near the university in

Grenoble

737. Playing the pinball machine in Dave Turkel's basement in 12th grade

738. Looking east from the I-195 overpass near Benefit St. in Providence during graduate school

739. The hideous train station in Florence during our big European trip

740. Sleeping with Cynthia Zarin at the edge of a soccer field at Domaine Université in Grenoble

741. The face of Professor Alan Heimert, my junior tutor and thesis adviser

742. Driving with Mom and Louisa from Austin airport on Martin Luther King Jr. Blvd. in '90

743. Noticing it was 90 degrees on the South Orange bank clock as the CHS tennis team returned from Summit

744. Waiting a long time for Dad to pick me up outside Dave Gurien's house in Maplewood

745. Walking with Mark Woldin past the Girl Scouts camp at the Res during a graduate-school vacation

746. The massive 19th century buildings on Genova's main drag during our honeymoon

747. Alice Lichtenstein's reading under the Brooklyn Bridge

748. Walking on Grove Rd. past a house that burned during high school

749. Looking westward down the tracks at the East Hampton train station

750. The Rijksmuseum during our trip to Amsterdam in '95

751. Carol Resnick's house on Tillou Rd. during junior high

752. Williamsburg Satmars walking on a bridge above the BQE in the early '90s

753. Going to the Claremont Diner in Verona during a college vacation

754. Playing on Cliff Greenberg's driveway in 6th grade

755. The train ride to Chester during my trip to Britain

756. The face of Dave Turkel

757. Drinking with Janet Murray at the jazz bar on Flatbush Ave. after the dance at BAM

758. Driving with Louisa and Owen Andrews to her childhood home in Haverford, Pa., on the last day of '85

759. Walking from Kate Brunet's apartment to Pere Lachaise to see

Apollinaire's grave

760. Playing stickball with Carl Adamo at Marshall School in 7th grade

761. Drinking Shirley Temples at a bar by the Club pool on a Memorial Day weekend

762. The time Dave Gurien and I hitched a ride with a slow driver and never made it to Mac Gander's house near Brattleboro in the summer after sophomore year

763. Driving under shady trees on the last stretch of the pre-I-280 drive to the Club

764. Feeling at the top of the world on a walk with Roland Vernon and Matt Wyatt in an upland pasture outside Chiusi during my year abroad

765. Eating pizza with my brother Steve near the Ossining psychiatric hospital where he received insulin-shock therapy in '72

766. Kate Augenblick's exhibit at Leslie Cecil Gallery on 72nd St. in the late '80s

767. Stopping for coffee along the jetty in Rockport on that fatal day, April 26, 1986

768. Waiting forever one day for a ride home from Bar Mitzvah practice at B'nai Jeshurun in 7th grade

769. Driving with Dad on the bridge over the Passaic River from Harrison to Newark

770. Exiting from the Prospect Expressway near Brooklyn's Greenwood Cemetery at night in the '90s

771. Driving with Bill Wood past the fruit stand near Ellsworth

772. Swimming in the narrow pool at the Tittmanns' house in Concord before Lili Porten and Jim Gussen's wedding in '91

773. Porn through a peephole in a soaped window on Wall Street during the Hill-Thomas hearings

774. Driving with Owen Andrews past a big retaining wall in Charlottesville in the summer after graduate school

775. Andy Newfeld's house on Summit Ave. in Maplewood during high school

776. The Brachmans' house in Columbus on the day of Lavea's wedding

777. Talking about Winter Harbor people with Owen Andrews during a visit back to Cambridge

778. Driving with Owen Andrews past that smoke-belching paper mill in Maine

779. Walking past the incongruous ranchhouse on Charlton Ave.

780. The Grassia Bros. fruit stand on Beacon St. in Somerville

781. Drinking boysenberry frappes with Emily Singer at Belgian Fudge in Harvard Square during junior year

782. The Mass. Ave. bus yard near Cameron Ave. during graduate school

783. Louisa's moneybelt breaking at the hotel a few hours before we were robbed outside Milan cathedral at the end of our honeymoon

784. Visiting the castle at the top of Enna during my trip to Sicily

785. The Cioppettini house on Centre St. on a cold night in 9th grade

786. Walking past the apple tree near Mrs. Lang's house on Raymond Ave.

787. Driving north on I-95 through Stanford, Conn., in the '90s

788. Leafletting Rutgers dorms for Tech Hifi

789. Driving with Miriam Smith past the Jewish Theological Seminary during my visit to Cincinnati in '88

790. Picking up Andy Freundlich to walk to school in 7th grade

791. Detouring through Quogue to avoid traffic on a drive home from the Hamptons

792. The sharp turn by the ancient sycamore near Bill Wood's farm in the mid-'90s

793. Waiting in the car outside an eyeglass store on Millburn Ave. in Maplewood during childhood

794. The tennis courts on Walton Ave. in Maplewood during high school

795. Playing tennis against West Essex High School in North Caldwell

796. The train station in Bethpage

797. The face of Mitchell Price during high school

798. Reading a Mickey Spillane novel in the hall outside Andy Newfeld's room during high school

799. Wondering if we were going to move away from Brooklyn during a sunset drive in Bay Ridge with one-year-old Charlotte asleep in the backseat

800. The green of the par 3 15th hole at the Club during a college summer vacation

801. Flood's Hill in springtime

802. Stopped at a light on Route 18 in New Brunswick where Dad had a costly accident five years before

803. Eating at Grace's, the burger place near the LIE on the way home from the Hamptons

804. Walking from Museum St. to Mac Gander's house on Leland St. during senior year

805. Driving past Irvington High on a summer evening on the way home from Tech Hifi

806. The Fontana dei Fiumi in Rome during our big European trip

807. The face of Steve Longo during childhood

808. The huge tree across the street from Columbia High

809. That skinny park along the East River at Houston St. during my New York walks

810. A hellish time finding our way back to the Thruway in Albany during our driving tour of the Northeast

811. Walking with Gary Lovesky to the old VA building near the Capitol in Providence

812. Grandma Gert on a Manhattan street in the '70s

813. Visiting our landlord's hardware store in Union Square in Somerville

814. The shady streets on the Orange side of Warwick Ave.

815. Driving past the school parking lot on the shortcut to Main Beach in East Hampton

816. The exhibit of Belgian modernists in Brussels during our big European trip

817. Walking alongside the jetty in Rockport on that fatal day, April 26, 1986

818. Sex with Cynthia Zarin on a mountainside in Aix les Bains during my year abroad

819. That heavy 19th century section of Florence, Piazza Republica, during our big European trip

820. The ladies shoe store in South Orange Village during childhood

821. The rhododendrons outside the 4th grade entrance to Marshall School

822. Pulling onto I-280 near Pal's Cabin during a college vacation

823. Walking past the original Tech Hifi store at MIT during college

824. Walking past the big memorial boulder in Grove Park

825. The weird Swedish girl with Jeff Holman at the East Hampton train station in '85

826. The wacky night when Dave Gurien and I took a ride with "Loony" and Ed Ublower and saw through their car's floorboards in 9th grade

827. The inside of South Orange train station in the summer after college graduation

828. South Orange Public Library during junior high

829. Grandma Gert's living room in the '70s

830. The green of the par 3 15th hole at the Club during a college summer vacation

831. That bank clock on the drive back from the CHS tennis match in Summit

832. Driving Louisa's fellow art-history graduate student to her parents' house near Manchester

833. Marc Lester running out of gas a mile from home on the drive back from the Adirondacks in 12th grade

834. Returning from that ecstatic walk outside Chiusi during my year abroad

835. Standing amid the rhododendrons outside the 4th grade entrance to Marshall School

836. The face of Mrs. Wolf, my high-school Latin teacher

837. Walking past a spooky Victorian house near Tanglewood on our first wedding anniversary

838. Driving past that octagonal church in Richmond near Lucy and Knox Cummin's house

839. Eating dinner with Mann Genchell at a restaurant near the Hudson River in '88

840. That boat trip with Uncle Milton and Aunt Miriam

841. That last stretch of the drive to Gary Lovesky's wedding on Route 128

842. Stopping with Dave Gurien at a tough Mexican bar as we hitched up the Pacific Coast Highway in the summer after junior year

843. Walking on Grove Rd. to Marshall School in 6th grade

844. Empty seltzer bottles on the steps to Matt Kassin's basement in 5th grade

845. Stopping to get Owen Andrews' car fixed on our first day in Nova Scotia

846. Driving with Owen Andrews in eastern West Virginia in '84

847. Walking near Gary Lovesky's apartment on Cameron Ave. in the fall after graduate school

848. Visiting a Brooklyn art gallery with my brother-in-law Billy Wood a few months ago, on April 9, 1997, the day after our twins were born

849. Standing outside the Uffizi during our big European trip

850. Hanging out with the Guriens at Steve Goldberg's house in 10th grade

851. That time the cops caught us throwing snowballs at cars at the VA hospital

852. The memorial trees planted at Marshall School

853. Visiting a mountain swimming hole in Vermont with Beth Duddy and Philip Mosenthal in '95

854. Playing basketball with Mac Gander that time he chipped my teeth

855. The face of Peter Grubstein from the Club

856. Reading Tony Eprile's book of stories at Garfield Pl. in the early '90s

857. Walking along the top of Flood's Hill

858. The face of Larry Hannawalt

859. The hypermarket where I bought the gas stove in Grenoble

860. The big turn as Pine St. enters Manchester

861. Being picked for the Little League majors by Rotary's Art Caplow in 4th grade

862. Sheep grazing on vertical green pastures at the top of the world in Skye during my trip to Britain

863. The face of Donny Wachenfeld from junior high

864. Walking past the mansion of Louisa's Auntie Louie in Georgetown in '86

865. A roadside restaurant in Pennsylvania on the way to my sister Alice's house in West Virginia in the mid-'90s

866. Dropping people off in West Orange during a carpool for indoor tennis or synagogue

867. Walking past Harry Zelnick's house during junior high

868. Driving home from I-280 on Valley Rd. in Orange during college or graduate school

869. Visiting Larry Hannawalt at his house in Cambridge

870. The spiral stairs at the Bessers' house in Vermont in 10th grade

870. The spiral stairs at the Bessers' house in Vermont in 10th grade

871. Looking up at the roof of Gary Lovesky's apartment on Cameron Ave.

872. The parking lot outside Pal's Cabin after Dad's 70th birthday party in '85

873. That corn plot near the tennis courts in Grenoble

874. The bus station in Perugia

875. Walking with Peter Baker in that big cemetery along the Seekonk River

876. Checking out a Massachusetts North Shore country club with Bill Wood and Mom the day we chose the rehearsal-dinner location for our wedding weekend

877. Heading north on Route 1 from Boston to Manchester or Maine

878. A magical afternoon at the Reillys' house on Warwick Ave. in 1st grade

879. Browsing at The Harvard Bookstore

880. Listening to David Bromberg's annual June concert at Eagle Rock

881. Stopping at the Baskin Robbins near Overbrook psychiatric hospital in Cedar Grove, N.J., during a college vacation

882. The spa at the Telluride ski area in '96

883. Driving to Manchester

884. Walking along Grove Terrace by the private road

885. Glenn Ruga's house in West Orange during high school

886. Reading Proust in the parking lot at Tech Hifi in East Brunswick

887. Watching a B&O train pass through Fort Kent during trip season at Kennebec senior

888. Rockport on that fatal day, April 26, 1986

889. The spa at the Telluride ski area

890. Waiting at a train station in Wales during my trip to Britain

891. The endless park across from the Royal Palace in Brussels during our big European trip

892. Driving on the Pulaski Skyway toward Newark during childhood

893. Walking around the duck pond by SOJH

894. The Pergamon Museum in East Berlin during our big European trip

895. The 4th grade entrance to Marshall School

896. Driving with Owen Andrews to pick up a rental car on the day before my wedding

897. A gloomy dinner at a French restaurant in Chelsea after Louisa's orals in '91

898. Tufts library in the summer after 11th grade

899. Driving to Herman's with Dad to buy camping equipment

900. Picking corn that time near the tennis courts in Grenoble

901. Walking with Mac Gander on Winter Hill in Somerville shortly before I moved to Providence

902. Walking on Montrose Ave. near Nancy Stern's house

903. Driving home from Jon Fried and Deena Shoshkes' house in Millburn during a visit back to New Jersey

904. Walking with Joe Zente on Centre St. in the winter of 6th grade

905. Gary Lovesky's house in Wayland in '90

906. That upland pasture in Chiusi during my year abroad

907. The Cioppetini house on Centre St., where Our House meetings were held in 9th grade

908. Driving with Dad on Route 18 into New Brunswick

909. Walking out of Penn Station Newark during a college vacation

910. Reading Rabbit, Run at home with pneumonia

911. The archaeological museum in Siracusa

912. Seeing Athol Fugard's "Valley Song" with Mark Woldin in Midtown in '96

913. Standing in front of Harvard's Lowell House

914. Walking to a pond from Owen Andrews' cabin outside Charlottesville in the summer after graduate school

915. Waiting to be picked up at Penn Station Newark during college

916. The Binswangers chasing the cook with a meat cleaver on parents' weekend at Kennebec junior

917. Driving past the huge Christmas tree at the state senator's mansion on Gregory Ave. in West Orange during childhood

918. Looking at shop windows in East Hampton with my brother John in mind in the early '90s

919. Eating dinner with Louisa at South Street Seaport after work in '90

920. Driving with Bill Wood and Owen Andrews to arrange for my wedding rental car

921. Gary Lovesky's house on Cameron Ave.

922. Waiting in the Res for Jeff Pownes to bring the pot he owed me in 8th grade

923. Walking to Mark Woldin's house on Raymond Ave. during the last years of Dad's life

924. Eating lunch with Beth Duddy and Philip Mosenthal at a big outdoor party in Middlebury on a boiling day in '95

925. Getting drunk on white wine on the rocks with Louisa in Cinque Terre during our honeymoon

926. My unsuccessful attempt to get caddying work in the summer after high-school graduation

927. The Cioppetini house on Centre St. on a cold night in 9th grade

928. Stopping to look at that weedlot with Cynthia Zarin in Providence

929. Sitting with Louisa and our three little girls on the lawn at Tanglewood during my paternity leave for the twins

930. Driving from South Egremont, Mass., to Hudson, N.Y., on a rainy and fateful day after our first anniversary

931. Outside a Seals and Crofts or Kris Kristofferson concert at Seton Hall in 9th grade

932. Driving with Dad to Sunfish Pond in 9th grade

933. Standing on the north side of the CHS athletic fields

934. Seeing the Etruscan caves under Perugia through a bus window

935. Walking up the dogwood path on Flood's Hill during the last years of Dad's life

936. Talking about Knox Cummin in North Adams, Mass., during our driving tour of the Northeast

937. Wandering around the royal palace in Oslo, wondering about the King of Norway, during our big European trip

938. Walking with Dave Turkel past the main MIT buildings on Mass Ave. during freshman year

939. That time I ran to escape from a group of muggers in New Brunswick

940. Returning the way-overdue copy of Fyodor Dostoevsky's Raw Youth to the Maplewood library in 12th grade

941. Looking at Stu Richter's little home greenhouse in Maplewood in 10th

grade

942. Eating with Emily Singer at the Noho Star in '90

943. Playing tennis against Matt Waldor during high school

944. Mom and Dad talking of separation at Harvard Motor Inn during freshmen parents' weekend

945. Walking hurriedly on a Boston street to Owen and Eleanor Andrews' rehearsal dinner

946. The beginning of a wonderful drive across northern Vermont last summer, in August '97

947. Driving on Route 9 looking at houses in Hastings, N.Y., in '95

948. Passing history teacher David Hogenauer's house in Maplewood in 12th grade

949. Getting caught by the cops for camping near Hemlock Falls in the Res in 8th grade

950. Playing basketball with my stepbrother, Russ Pearce, at Lincoln playground in Brooklyn in the early '90s

951. Standing in the parking lot at the old deer paddock in the Res at the beginning of memory

952. Walking east on the Montrose Ave. bridge over Mountain Station

953. Sleeping with Cynthia Zarin behind a huge tree at the edge of that soccer field in Grenoble

954. Playing golf with Mom on a public course in northern Jersey during graduate school

955. The New Brunswick train station a couple of blocks from Tech Hifi

956. The entrance to Lowell House at Harvard

957. A sleepy moment of content riding home from a holiday meal in Manhattan during childhood

958. Parking in front of the nice frame house in Rockport on that fatal day, April 26, 1986

959. Handing in my Rotary uniform at the end of a Little League season

960. Playing in the brook behind the police station near Mark Woldin's house during junior high

961. The Italian fountains at Longwood Gardens in Pennsylvania any Easter from '86 to '96

962. Reading Nadine Gordimer's <u>A World of Strangers</u> at Garfield Pl. in the early '90s

963. Walking with Dave Gurien and his Allman Brothers friend all the way from the VA hospital in East Orange to Phil Carson's house in Maplewood in 10th grade

964. That boat trip with Uncle Milton and Aunt Miriam

965. The house of Keith Roberts and Steve Peckarsky in 5th grade

966. A train ride from South Orange to New York with Cynthia Zarin and Gary Lovesky during the fateful Christmas vacation of '82

967. Walking up that curving panoramic road above the university in Perugia

968. The memorial trees at Marshall School

969. The face of Elise Paschen from Harvard

970. Walking through MIT with Owen Andrews and the baby Charlotte on the second day of '95

971. The first glimpse of Peconic Bay off Sebonac Rd. during a drive to the Hamptons

972. Looking across the CHS athletic fields

973. Driving in the Italian section of Providence during graduate school

974. Walking from the New Brunswick train station to Tech Hifi

975. A disturbing ride in a golf cart with Steve Davimos at the Club in the summer after junior year, the last time I ever saw my childhood friend

976. Playing touch football with David Wiesman in gym in 7th grade

977. Looking at that Victorian house near Tanglewood

978. The brook behind the police station during junior high

979. Walking from Sally Wood's Spiral Stairs condo to a shop in Telluride in '96

980. Driving up the Palisades Parkway to Beth Duddy and Philip Mosenthal's house in Harriman, N.Y., in the early '90s

981. Sitting in the small quad across from the John Hay Libary at Brown

982. The third-base line near the concrete-and-pipe fence at the Little League majors field

983. Driving with a Polish guide to Auschwitz during our big European trip

984. Looking at a house in Scarsdale, N.Y., in '96

985. Catching a bus to Gubbio at the station in Perugia

986. Playing tennis with Peter Brodie at Seton Hall during junior high

987. Driving past Brooklyn's Clinton Hill in the '80s or '90s

988. Peter Baker's house during a visit back to Providence

989. Leafletting New Brunswick high rises for Tech Hifi

990. Wandering around with Mark and Danny Woldin, clutching handfuls of stolen pot, after the famous party at Peter Kearny's house in 8th grade

991. That big turn as Pine St. enters Manchester late at night

992. That crabapple tree across Prospect St. from Dr. Shire's office during the last years of Dad's life

993. The sculpture garden at the L.A. County Museum in '96

994. A street in Belgium during our big European trip

995. Waiting with Bill Wood at a red light in Villanova after "The Shootout at the Prozac Corral" in '95

996. Buying camp clothes for Kennebec at Bellin's

997. An uncomfortable afternoon with Owen and Eleanor Andrews at the Boston Arboretum in '93

998. Dr. Leo Kohn's waiting room in South Orange during childhood

999. A decrepit Borromini church in Rome during our big European trip

1000. Eating lunch by a fountain and waiting for Monreale to reopen during my trip to Sicily

1001. Sitting on a park bench near the Educational Alliance on East Broadway in the early '90s

1002. Visiting the Verrier's house with Peter Baker in Avignon during my year abroad

1003. Going to an old-fashioned Christmas movie at Maplewood Theater during childhood

1004. The last blocks of Benefit St. before the Star Market in Providence

1005. Mac Gander writing a poem about a blue swallow during a walk in Vermont in '81

1006. Sleeping with Cynthia Zarin by that soccer field in Grenoble

1007. That time the cops caught us throwing snowballs at cars at the VA hospital

1008. Discussing Seamus Heaney with Owen Andrews and Cynthia Zarin during a walk past mansions on Brattle St. in Cambridge

1009. A huge party suddenly arriving at a sleepy seafood place in Catania during my trip to Sicily

1010. A scary drive with Owen Andrews to Lowell during a visit back to Cambridge

1011. Walking with my brother Steve past the Maplewood train station in the spring of '95

1012. The gardens at Tanglewood during my paternity leave

1013. Walking across the parking lot where the CHS frisbee team played

1014. Reading Rabbit, Run at home with pneumonia

1015. Driving south at night on the BQE to Tillary St. in Brooklyn

1016. Looking at the Nathans' greenhouse from the Brodies' backyard during childhood

1017. Walking up that curving panoramic road to our pizzeria in Perugia

1018. Standing with Cynthia Zarin in front of Jane Shore's old house in Cambridge

1019. Playing catch with Joe Zente in the melting snow in the next-door neighbor's yard

1020. The main square in Bologna during our honeymoon

1021. Nat Gurien's house at the Jersey shore in December '97

1022. That peepshow on Wall Street during the Hill-Thomas hearings

1023. The big cemetery at the end of Blackstone Blvd. in Providence

1024. Turning in my Rotary uniform at the community house after a Little League season

1025. Seeing Michelangelo's David for the first time in 12 years during our big European trip

1026. Walking back from playing golf at Fresh Pond at the beginning of freshman year

1027. That skinny park along FDR Drive at Houston St. during my New York walks

1028. Seeing my niece Abby Travis play bass with "The Love Dolls" at Maxwell's in Hoboken in '87

1029. Going with Louisa and Kate Brunet to Musée Marmattan

1030. The house with big sycamores on Montrose Ave. that was painted during early childhood

1031. Going to Debby Smith's house during my visit to Cincinnati

1032. Walking up Jamie Siegel's shady driveway in Maplewood in 11th grade

1033. The tree with huge bumps and squirrel holes between our house and the Brodie house

1034. Walking near Cameron Field in South Orange

1035. Walking with Billy Wood to get dinner on Atlantic Ave. in Brooklyn a day after the twins' birth

1036. Putting the canoe in the Winooski River with Lucy and Knox Cummin

1037. Driving past Rock Spring Country Club in West Orange

1038. Waiting on the eastbound platform at South Orange station during the last years of Dad's life

1039. Going with Dad to visit my brother Steve at Overbrook psychiatric hospital during a college vacation

1040. Driving past that octagonal church in Richmond near Lucy and Knox Cummin's house

1041. A rock concert at Upsala during junior high

1042. Stopping for ice cream at Welsh Farms on the way home from the Club

1043. Playing tennis with Jon Fried at Harvard Business School in the fall after college graduation

1044. Walking across the Mass. Ave. bridge from Boston during college

1045. The Greyhound counter at Penn Station Newark in the early '80s

1046. That lunch with Beth Duddy and Philip Mosenthal on a boiling day in Middlebury

1047. That apple tree near Dad's apartment house during the last years of his life

1048. Walking home across the Brooklyn Bridge with Ezra Palmer

1049. The face of Scott Solis in Shakespeare class at graduate school

1050. Walking on Atlantic Ave. in '90

1051. Crossing that bridge over the Huntington River in Vermont

1052. Walking west up Irving Ave.

1053. Joe Zente's house on Holland Rd.

1054. Turning left from Hands Creek Rd. onto Cedar Lane in East Hampton

1055. Driving Louisa's art-history colleague to her parents' house

1056. Andrea Mentzel's father giving me a ride home that night in 9th grade

1057. A wide hallway in the Louvre during my year abroad

1058. Hiking with Dave Gurien at Bear Mt. during high school

1059. The swings near Lili Porten and Jim Gussen's apartment during a visit back to Cambridge

1060. That powwow with Matt Waldor in the Stillmans' backyard after college graduation

1061. Meeting Lavea Brachman outside the Art Institute of Chicago during a visit to my sister Liz

1062. Entering Tufts library in the summer after 11th grade

1063. The zipper repair shop in Budapest during our big European trip

1064. Buying cocktail napkins as a Christmas present for Mom during childhood

1065. Mark Woldin's garden party celebrating his Rutgers graduation in '82

1066. Exploring downtown Brooklyn with Owen Andrews during my New York walks

1067. The face of Andy Freundlich from South Orange

1068. Picking corn that time near the tennis courts in Grenoble

1069. Driving to Manchester from Boston

1070. The last stretch of Noyack Rd. before Route 27 in the Hamptons

1071. Bathing with Cynthia Zarin in a crappy lake in western Jersey

1072. Discussing Charles Olson with Owen Andrews in downtown Brooklyn's Cadmon Plaza

1073. The hotel room in Venice during our honeymoon trip

1074. A cold walk with the baby Charlotte at Bill Wood's farm

1075. Spying on an Atlantis Sound store for Tech Hifi in East Brunswick

1076. Crossing the Hudson River at Catskill during our driving tour of the Northeast

1077. Taking our three girls to a sleepy playground near Tanglewood during my paternity leave

1078. Dressing for a long hike on a frigid day with Chuck Schwartz in Williamsville

1079. Avoiding saying hello to my brother John while waiting for Lavea Brachman on 72nd St. in '85

1080. That doctor's office on South Orange Ave. near Joe Zente's house

1081. Driving downhill past Danny Sarewitz's house during junior high

1082. Picking up the rental car with Bill Wood and Owen Andrews on the day before my wedding

1083. Meredith Kamen's house in Newstead

1084. Hiking on rocks at Bear Mt. during high school

1085. That peepshow on Wall Street during the Hill-Thomas hearings

1086. A train ride from Milan to Bologna during our honeymoon

1087. Hiking down from Sunfish Pond on a visit back to western Jersey in '85

1088. The face of Andrea Mentzel

1089. Driving over the Charlestown Bridge from Boston to Manchester

1090. People scrubbing graffiti off the wall by the girls' gym entrance at SOJH

1091. Walking with Peter Baker, Gary Lovesky and Manya Daner past a psychiatric hospital in Providence on a frigid day in the late '80s

1092. The decrepit backstop of the girls' softball field at Marshall School

1093. The first glimpse of Peconic Bay off Sebonac Rd. during a drive to the Hamptons

1094. A street in Chamonix during my year abroad

1095. Watching a truck being painted with Chinese letters in Brooklyn's Gowanus during my New York walks

1096. Climbing to the tower on Winter Hill with Owen Andrews during a visit back to Cambridge

1097. Peter Baker telling someone that I "didn't know one word of French" in Avignon during my year abroad

1098. Grove Rd. in front of the Rohde house

1099. Walking up 3rd St. to Ridgewood Rd. in South Orange

1100. Parking by a lookout at the Res while Mom was getting a root canal in '95

1101. My golfball hitting the big tree over the 18th fairway at the Club during a college vacation

1102. That seafood restaurant in Catania

1103. Driving with Louisa in the country near Beverly, Mass.

1104. Sitting on a stone wall with Louisa during a walk in Manchester

1105. Reading Anton Chekov's "A Boring Story" in the late '80s

1106. The house with a weird insect-killing light near Cheselyn Amato's house during high school

1107. Leaving the South Orange Public Library by the back entrance

1108. Walking along the broad Cours Jean Jaurés in Grenoble

1109. Shopping with Cynthia Zarin at Boston's Haymarket

1110. Walking north on Museum St. past the Divinity School during a visit back to Cambridge

1111. The 6th Ave. Deli near Grandma Gert's apartment during childhood

1112. The fancy restaurant at the corner of Kirkland St. and Beacon St. in Cambridge before college graduation

1113. Cutting school and going to the Res with a vial of "orange sunshine" in 8th grade

1114. The Stillmans' first house in Maplewood

1115. Crossing the train trestle near Mountain Station with Patty Lafferty in 9th grade

1116. The beech copse with mayapples beyond the fields at Bill Wood's farm

1117. An elementary school in Brooklyn's Carroll Gardens during my New York walks

1118. Andy Freundlich's new icemaker in 7th grade

1119. The Paul Newman poster above the pool table in Steve Kurens' basement

1120. Christmas dinner with Dad at Mayfair Farm near Eagle Rock during the last years of his life

1121. The big view on the drive to New Lebanon, N.Y., from Pittsfield, Mass., during my paternity leave

1122. Uncle Milton talking about his dead brother, Uncle Leslie Handler, in Westhampton in '91

1123. A ritzy house at the corner of Ralston Ave. and Charlton Ave.

1124. My brother David's friends Kenny Citron and Richard Zemel by the tennis courts in 9th grade

1125. Driving home from Orange along Scotland Rd.

1126. Walking north on Museum St. past the Divinity School during a visit back to Cambridge

1127. Walking to that park near Lili Porten and Jim Gussen's apartment in Cambridge

1128. The poet James Wright smoking alone in Harvard's Boylston Hall in the fall after college graduation

1129. Walking to the beach at Scheverningen during our big European trip

1130. Sitting on a ledge with Cynthia Zarin looking at Mt. Blanc across the Vale of Chamonix

1131. Eating dinner with Sharon Frost in Williamsburg in the mid-'90s

1132. The ice-skating house at the duck pond by SOJH

1133. Norma Ziegler's mother's apartment on Valley St. during high school

1134. Looking at that book at MIT that cited my brother Sandy's research

1135. Playing football at Grove Park with Chuck Schwartz a year before his death in '80

1136. Seeing Jamie Gowan by the big dock in Northeast Harbor in '93

1137. Pickerel weed around the docks of the counselors' cottages at Kennebec senior

1138. Walking with Owen Andrews in Brooklyn's Boerum Hill during my New York walks

1139. Getting a Coke at the South Orange community center after CHS tennis practice

1140. Driving with Bill Wood by that fruit stand in Ellsworth

1141. The funny eye-shaped windows on the roofs in Budapest during our big European trip

1142. Gulf War yellow ribbons on trees near Beth Duddy and Philip Mosenthal's house in Harriman

1143. The pond near Owen Andrews' cabin outside Charlottesville in the summer after graduate school

1144. Talking with Owen Andrews on a Roanoke railroad bridge on a boiling day in '86

1145. The soda machine at the Sunoco station near SOJH

1146. Visiting PepsiCo's sculpture park in Purchase with Louisa and one-year-old Charlotte

1147. Walking with Bea Bindman through Memorial Park in 11th grade

1148. Doing "corporate espionage" for Tech Hifi in New Brunswick

1149. Steve Weis's house during graduate school

1150. Eating out with Dad and Dale Schulty in Ann Arbor in the summer after graduate school

1151. A long cross-country ski with Lucy and Knox Cummin in January '93, our last visit to Huntington

1152. Streets near Chuck Schwartz's house in Maplewood during high school

1153. That little basketball court on Beacon St. in Somerville

1154. The water-pumping station at Grove Park during a visit back to South Orange

1155. Watching kids play football at Grove Park in the fall after college graduation

1156. Wolfing down a cornetto con crema at the train station in Palermo during my trip to Sicily

1157. My dream about a Mexican boy and a party for arms dealers in the mid-'90s

1158. Walking up Raymond Ave. to Mrs. Lang's house, where Mark Woldin lived on and off from '75 to '93

1159. Driving on the Garden State Parkway to Tech Hifi in New Brunswick

1160. A martinet L.A. cop directing traffic on the day of the Northridge earthquake

1161. Walking out of the archaeological museum in Siracusa

1162. Getting off the Blue Route near Billy and Molly Wood's house in Villanova, Pa., in the mid-'90s

1163. Going to Rumpelmayer's on Central Park South with my sister Liz during high school

1164. Walking by that apple tree on Raymond Ave.

1165. Picking up sandwiches for everyone at the New Brunswick Tech Hifi store

1166. Driving on the Beltway at night to visit Owen Andrews in Harrisonburg, Va., in '84

1167. The green tent that Cynthia Zarin and I used in Aix les Bains

1168. Reading 17th century poetry and eating chicken soup in a teacher lounge at East Boston High

1169. A huge slag pile in Wales during my trip to Britain

1170. That time Keith Roberts hit me in the head with an iceball in 6th grade

1171. Driving to the Claremont Diner late at night during a college vacation

1172. My sister Kathy talking about John Ashbery on Mass. Ave. in Cambridge during freshman year

1173. A warm fall day in Ostia Antica during our big European trip

1174. Walking with Owen and Eleanor Andrews over the bridge from East Cambridge to Charlestown

1175. Sitting in Steve Weis's living room during graduate school

1176. Driving the last stretch of Route 3 into Ellsworth earlier this year, in August '98

1177. Driving with my senior tutor Prudence Steiner to pick up hors d'oeuvres after college graduation

1178. Mark Woldin introducing me to Chris Murtagh in South Orange Village in the summer after college graduation

1179. Looking at Doc Humes' old apartment on Western Ave. during a trip back to Cambridge

1180. Driving in the Brooklyn-Battery Tunnel in the mid-'90s

1181. Flirting with Tanya Luhrmann on the train from Boston to New York during sophomore year

1182. Parking with Louisa and Owen Andrews by the Air and Space Museum in Washington in '90

1183. The crowded A&P parking lot in East Hampton at night

1184. Climbing up Bear Mt. with Andrew Gurien during high school

1185. The ice-cream place at a driving range on Route 27 in Southampton in the early '80s

1186. The soda machine in the South Orange community center

1187. Driving through Orange Park to my brother Steve's room at the Y during a college vacation

1188. Hitting a double in stickball at Marshall School

1189. That night at Andrea Mentzel's in 9th grade

1190. Stopping at Lee Schwartz's in East Hampton earlier this year, in July '98

1191. Mountain climbers walking through Chamonix during my year abroad

1192. Telling Eleanor Tittmann about Dad's death at Singing Beach in Manchester

1193. Buying breakfast with Randy Blair at the Broadway Deli in Bethpage

1194. Looking at the bell tower at the entrance to Cornell in the summer after college graduation

1195. Eating at a restaurant with Susan Ei and her friends on Route 27 in Napeague in '92

1196. Looking at the Oheb Shalom parking lot from Mrs. Lang's backyard

1197. The leafy neighborhood in Berlin near the Brucke museum during our big European trip

1198. The "Indian reservation" with the "refrigerator" at Kennebec junior

1199. Spying on Atlantis Sound for Tech Hifi

1200. Dave Gurien's father's apartment in Arlington

1201. Victorian houses in Lebanon Springs during my paternity leave

1202. Crossing train tracks near MIT with Owen Andrews during a visit back to Cambridge

1203. The garage of our next-door neighbor's house on Hartford Rd.

1204. Walking under I-195 to the Rhode Island Fish Co. store during graduate school

1205. The face of Andrea Mentzel

1206. Walking with Owen Andrews around Philadelphia on the last day of '85

1207. Driving past the famous Zwillman house in Maplewood

1208. Driving on the south side of Bloomfield Park

1209. Leaving Fran Nathan's apartment on 89th St. after a Thanksgiving dinner during college

1210. Marveling with Chuck Schwartz at all the new snow out the window in Williamsville

1211. Our car exiting from the Garden State Parkway onto Route 3 East during childhood

1222. That afternoon at the Reilly house on Warwick Ave. in 1st grade

1223. Rita Fava picking us up at the church with the great Caravaggios, Santa Maria del Popolo in Rome, during our big European trip

1224. Looking out a bus window at the Etruscan caves under Perugia

1225. Driving on a curving road near Fresh Pond during college

1226. Walking past a viburnum by Marshall School during the last years of Dad's life

1227. A flash flood at Cameron Field in 8th grade

1228. Walking around MIT with Owen Andrews during a visit back to Cambridge

1229. Eating at a Tex-Mex restaurant with Sandy Stillman on West St. in the mid-'80s

1230. Leaving the Bologna train station with Louisa during our honeymoon

1231. Driving with Knox Cummin from Montauk Point to East Hampton in the late '80s

1232. Walking through woods to the Stockbridge Bowl on our first anniversary

1233. Looking at a house with a widow's walk in Rockport on that fatal day, April 26, 1986

1234. The shady playground at Marshall School during a visit back to South Orange

1235. Driving in the Battery Tunnel

1236. Marc Lester's car stuck in the mud in the Adirondacks in 12th grade

1237. The Frank Lloyd Wright tour in Oak Park during a visit to my sister Liz in Chicago

1238. The big maple in front of Marshall School

1239. Sitting alone on a hill in Harrisonburg

1240. Hearing about the Shah's death with Cynthia Zarin in Annecy

1241. The Marlboro Bookstore on 57th and 7th near Grandma Gert's apartment in 11th grade

1242. That hedge topped by spiderwebs in Grenoble

1243. Norma Ziegler's mother's apartment on Valley St.

1244. Brooklyn's Carroll Gardens during my New York walks

1245. Uncle Milton and Aunt Miriam's boat

1246. Walking from Kate Brunet's apartment to Pere Lachaise on a gray day

1247. That fancy restaurant on Kirkland St. and Beacon St. around college graduation

1248. Passing the drive-in theater on Route 10 during early childhood

1249. Sitting with Cynthia Zarin and a Yugoslavian couple at our campsite in Chamonix

1250. That party at the seafood restaurant in Catania

1251. Stopping at a fruit store on the way home to Western Ave. in Cambridge during junior year

1252. Waiting for the train at East Hampton station

1253. Sitting with Mark Woldin on a hillside in the Res during the last years of Dad's life

1254. Walking up 3rd St. toward Ridgewood Rd. in South Orange

1255. Rick Spiers in front of Widener Library during sophomore year

1256. Driving on Old House Landing Rd. to Sammis Beach Rd. in East Hampton in the '90s

1257. Sex with Mylene Hodgson at the Audubon sanctuary in Fairfield, Conn., in '84

1258. The face of Cheryl Dunsker from South Orange

1259. Sandy Stillman's house in Ithaca in the summer after college graduation

1260. Hearing about the Shah's death with Cynthia Zarin in Annecy

1261. Looking at the Oheb Shalom parking lot from Mrs. Lang's backyard

1262. Walking past the VEGE store on my street in Perugia

1263. Fishing tires out of the mud with Boy Scouts in western Jersey in 7th grade

1264. The house with its shades permanently drawn on Vose Ave. and Mead St.

1265. Finding the pot plant with Dave Turkel near Pathmark

1266. That doctor's office on South Orange Ave. near Joe Zente's house

1267. Walking up the path through the dogwoods on Flood's Hill during the last years of Dad's life

1268. Ordering Rob Roys with Mark Woldin at Stuffed Shirt in the summer after high-school graduation

1269. Looking at Vincent Van Gogh's "Starry Night" at the Met retrospective in the late '80s

1270. The block of Ralston Ave. between Grove Park and Mark Woldin's house

1271. Mt. Auburn Cemetery on a misty day during a visit back to Cambridge

1272. Reading The Tale of Genji in our house at 433 4th St. in Brooklyn in '98

1273. Waiting for Ben Blackmer at a recording studio during my visit to Cincinnati

1274. The face of Bill Wood's friend Charlie Grimes

1275. Walking in a Baltimore alley with Peter Baker in '98

1276. Walking along a Leiden canal during our big European trip

1277. Turning east from Court St. onto Union St. in Brooklyn

1278. The girls' softball diamond at Marshall School

1279. A roadside café in some movie

1280. A bicyclist riding away from a prostitute in the Bois de Boulogne in '95

1281. Jeff Holman waiting at the East Hampton train station

1282. Stopping for soft ice cream in Montauk with Lucy Cummin in '90

1283. Psilocybin mushrooms at Steve Weis's house during graduate school

1284. Playing tennis with my brother-in-law Larry Travis at an L.A. club during a college summer vacation

1285. Meeting Jimmy Gander at his CETA job in Brattleboro in the fall after college graduation

1286. Walking downhill from Donny Wachenfeld's house in 8ᵗʰ grade

1287. That old-fashioned mailbox on Charlton Ave.

1288. Vienna's overgrown Jewish cemetery on a freezing day during our big European trip

1289. Dad falling during a business visit to the Tigers' octagonal house near Eagle Rock in 8ᵗʰ grade

1290. Hitting tennis balls against the wall at the B'nai Jeshurun parking lot in 5ᵗʰ grade

1291. Sitting on an outcrop with Gary Lovesky at the Fellsway in the fall after graduate school

1292. Walking to the Brucke museum in Berlin during our big European trip

1293. Riding the camp bus from Logan Airport to Kennebec junior

1294. The carwash on Broadway in Somerville that Mac Gander wrote about in '81

1295. Walking along the outer edge of the Jewish cemetery in Vienna

1296. Walking with Janet Murray in Mt. Lebanon Shaker village during my paternity leave

1297. The parking lot at Pal's Cabin

1298. Gordon Boggie's Airedale in 4ᵗʰ grade

1299. Going with Dave Gurien to a painful party at Gary Lehr's house in 11th grade

1300. Looking at houses with Louisa and two-year-old Charlotte in the Edgemont section of Scarsdale

1301. Talking about my work at the *Journal* with Bill and Sally Wood on a drive to the races in Maryland in the early '90s

1302. Walking across the bridge toward the Narragansett Electric Plant during graduate school

1303. Queechy Lake in the Berkshires during my paternity leave

1304. Sandy Stillman pointing out a Spanish restaurant in the West Village during my New York walks

1305. Taking the train to East Orange for Mr. Pantazes' SAT practice course during high school

1306. Reading Nathaniel Hawthorne's Fanshawe in Winter Harbor in '95

1307. Driving with Bill Wood past the big Scott Paper plant on Washington's Birthday in '95, exactly a year before his death

1308. Going out for pizza with Mom and Eli in Southampton

1309. Driving with Bill Wood through West Chester, Pa., during the last years of his life

1310. Taking French at Harvard Extension School two years after college graduation

1311. Hanging out with Mylene Hodgson at a "Cucumbers" concert at a New York club in '84

1312. Sitting in the grass above the Hippodrome in Rome during our big European trip

1313. Taking our three little girls to the Brooklyn Children's Museum

1314. Accidentally eating a burger with Neal Besser in Stowe, Vt., in 10th grade

1315. Looking at an outcrop near Mac Gander's old place during a visit back to Somerville

1316. The memorial rock in Grove Park

1317. Talking to Louisa's cousin Sonia Wieder-Atherton after her cello concert in Paris in '95

1318. Seeing Albany in the distance during our driving tour of the Northeast

1319. Walking on that broad 19th century street in Genova during our honeymoon

1320. Huddled with a British couple, Jose and Frances, during a thunderstorm on the coast of Stromboli during my trip to Sicily

1321. Skating on the duck pond by SOJH during early childhood

1322. The indoor gardens at Longwood the day after Bill Wood's funeral

1323. The face of Uncle Milton

1324. Talking to that Yugoslavian couple in Chamonix during my year abroad

1325. Running into Liz Bernstein on Mass. Ave. in Cambridge a couple of years after college graduation

1326. The face of Henry Hersch from Kennebec

1327. Looking at the quote on the ceiling of the Library of Congress reading room with Peter Baker and Louisa in '92

1328. Getting picked up by Deena Shoshkes and Jon Fried at the Bethpage printing plant

1329. The ruined deer paddock at the Res during the last years of Dad's life

1330. Walking past embassies on a cold day in Kensington during our trip to London

1331. Driving on Route 128 to Gary Lovesky's wedding

1332. Walking with Helmut in the boulder field in the Alps near Grenoble

1333. Making out with Debby Mortimer in Dave Gurien's backyard in 10th grade

1334. Driving over the bridge out of Sag Harbor in the early evening in the '90s

1335. Listening to Frank Zappa at the Ribots' house in 8th grade

1336. The outside of Knox Cummin's first sculpture studio in Philadelphia in the late '80s

1337. Hitching a ride out of the Sierras in a steamy car with George Kane during my cross-country trip

1338. "Uncle Si" Dunklee at a campsite during trip season at Kennebec senior

1339. Driving to a farm near Stockbridge to buy peach jam at the beginning of memory

1340. Waking at Dave Turkel's MIT frat house after a night of tripping during freshman year

1341. Meeting Janet Murray for dinner in Tribeca with Louisa and the baby

Charlotte

1342. Standing under the sycamores in front of the South Orange tennis courts

1343. Sitting with Dave Gurien on the roadside at Smuggler's Notch in Vermont in the summer after sophomore year

1344. Those empty seltzer bottles on the steps to Matt Kassin's basement in 5th grade

1345. Our one-year-old twins sleeping in the car on Main St. in Geneseo, N.Y.

1346. The dusty tennis courts across the brook from SOJH

1347. Susan Manno and Alexander Wood in Dianne B's backyard in East Hampton a few months after the twins' birth

1348. Riding with Bob Brennan in the van home from the *Journal*

1349. That corn plot near the tennis courts in Grenoble

1350. Driving past a candy store in East Orange during childhood

1351. Eating with Knox Cummin at a Chinese restaurant near his second studio in the early '90s

1352. Walking around my brother Sandy's neighborhood in Milton on a snowy day

1353. Driving with Peter Baker to the Towson campus in '98

1354. Seeing the James Bond movie "Thunderball" during childhood

1355. Throwing snowballs at cars on South Orange Ave. with Brian Molloy in 5th grade

1356. Driving past Bernheim-Goldsticker Funeral Home in Irvington, where my brother David's funeral took place

1357. That visit with Dad to the Tiger's octagonal house

1358. Dave Gurien's apartment in San Francisco at the time of his wedding in '92

1359. Kissing Sharon Mastrangelo on the grass at night on Ralston Ave. in 8th grade

1360. Driving past a kitschy restaurant shaped like an ocean liner on Route 22 during childhood

1361. Walking downhill to Mama Rondolini's apartment, the first place I lived in Perugia

1362. Those mushrooms at Steve Weis's house

1363. Talking with the Yugoslavians in Chamonix

1364. Hurrying from one Boston bus station to another to meet Louisa in '85

1365. Fourth of July fireworks in South Orange during early childhood

1366. Mrs. Lang's backyard on Raymond Ave.

1367. Teeing off on the steep 8th hole at the Club during a college vacation

1368. Noticing the head shop in New Lebanon during my paternity leave

1369. Doing dishes at the Zarins' house in Wellfleet, Mass., in the summer after college graduation

1370. Taking the boat from Camp Androscoggin on the trip back to Kennebec senior

1371. Making out with Cheselyn Amato in the overgrown vacant lot on Vose Ave. in 12th grade

1372. Parking with Peter Baker in his old Baltimore neighborhood in '98

1373. That hedge topped by spiderwebs in Grenoble

1374. Driving on Route 128 to my brother Sandy's wedding in Milton in '82

1375. Crossing above the Mass Pike in West Stockbridge during my paternity leave

1376. Hiking through woods on the Appalachian Trail in western Jersey during high school

1377. Going to a bar on the far side of Tufts in the summer after 11th grade

1378. Wandering through a thrift shop in Bethpage after missing the train back to New York

1379. A boiling day with Knox Cummin in Brooklyn's Gowanus during my New York walks

1380. Entering the Children's Museum with my three girls earlier this year, in January '99

1381. Walking home along a factory wall near Mac Gander's apartment on Leland St. during senior year

1382. A cold bench near the palace in Vienna during our big European trip

1383. The lights of the Chinese restaurant below Kate Brunet's apartment in Belleville

1384. Looking at the porches of houses on the north side of Winter Hill in Somerville

1385. Sitting with Cynthia Zarin and John Weiser in the kitchen of our apartment on 119 Museum St.

1386. Walking by the Orson Welles movie theater in Cambridge

1387. Stopping at a rest stop on the southbound side of the Jersey Turnpike in the '90s

1388. Fourth of July fireworks in South Orange during early childhood

1389. Running into Cynthia Zarin on the way to see "Veronica Voss" with Mylene Hodgson at Broadway and 96th St.

1390. Seeing Gilbert and Sullivan at Longwood Gardens during my paternity leave for Charlotte in June '94

1391. The motorcyle shop near Baskin Robbins in Harvard Square

1392. Pollarded trees on Via XX Settembre leading steeply up to Perugia's centro

1393. Hitching a ride at night from two priests on I-95 with "Uncle Jim" Mayer during trip season at Kennebec senior

1394. Brooklyn's Gowanus Houses during my New York walks

1395. Riding down the elevator in my apartment building on the outskirts of Grenoble

1396. Andy Newfeld, with a Spillane paperback in his back pocket, on the top floor of his house during high school

1397. Playing stickball at the basketball court at Marshall School

1398. Sitting with Mark Woldin by the duck pond, waiting for acid to take effect, in 8th grade

1399. Those mushrooms at Steve Weis's house

1400. Walking across the bridge on Beacon St. toward Porter Square in Cambridge

1401. Walking with Mom and Dad to a quiche place on Boylston St. in Cambridge during senior year

1402. Walking with Louisa and the baby Charlotte along the Orange border during a visit back to South Orange

1403. Waiting for Ben Blackmer at that Cincinnati recording studio

1404. Samuel Tilden's grave at New Lebanon's cemetery during my paternity leave for the twins

1405. The cobblestone road where I-280 used to peter out in Harrison in the '80s

1406. Talking to Dr. Giannotto with Mark Woldin during a visit back to South Orange

1407. Waiting by the train tracks with Gino near Lake Trasimeno during my year abroad

1408. Driving home past Tabatchnik's on Irvington Ave. during childhood

1409. Driving on the Palisades Parkway in the late '90s

1410. Golden Gate park in '83 or '92

1411. The waterfront in Brooklyn's Red Hook during my New York walks

1412. Checking out books about Nigeria at the Newark Public Library in 12th grade

1413. That afternoon at the Reillys' house on Warwick Ave. in 1st grade

1414. Getting Hebrides ferry schedules at the tourist office in Edinburgh during my trip to Britain

1415. Dancing on the grass with an injured heel at Lisa Kaufman's 6th grade graduation party

1416. Walking from Stockholm's palace to its opera house on a cold night during our big European trip

1417. Stopping to buy scotch as a gift for John Elson on Sunset Blvd. in '96

1418. Sue Straussberg's house on Hartford Ct.

1419. That apple tree near Mrs. Lang's house on Raymond Ave.

1420. Walking by Ginger Meehan's house on Ralston Ave. during junior high

1421. Hanging out with Dave Caplan outside Neal Besser's house on a frigid night in 9th grade

1422. Left for an endless hour with my baby sister Liz at Tanglewood's fountains at the beginning of memory

1423. Walking with Gary Lovesky in the dripping car tunnel under the Providence train station

1424. The row of dogwoods at Flood's Hill during the last years of Dad's life

1425. Turning right at the Mobil station at exit 70 on the LIE East

1426. Visiting a saltwater pool with my sister Alice and her boyfriend at the beginning of memory

1427. Walking with Mark Woldin past the town pool during a visit back to South Orange

1428. Driving past the Shinnecock Hills golf course in Southhampton

1429. The necktie section of the Harvard Coop

1430. The face of Todd Miller from the Club

1431. The Turner section of the Tate Gallery during our trip to London

1432. Walking with Knox Cummin past "the burnt coffee factory" in Brooklyn's Gowanus

1433. Waiting at Oban for the ferry to Mull during my trip to Britain

1434. Uncle Milton's lake in Yorktown Heights

1435. The dusty tennis courts across the brook from SOJH

1436. Walking with Helmut in the boulder field in the Alps near Grenoble

1437. The Uffizi Museum in '80 or '92

1438. Sitting with Louisa and Owen Andrews by the Hunnewell mausoleum at Mt. Auburn Cemetery during a visit back to Cambridge

1439. Crossing the green plastic bridge over South Orange Ave. in the Res

1440. Driving south past the woods across from E.J. Korvette

1441. Walking with Peter Baker in that big cemetery during a visit back to Providence

1442. That rental-car place the day before our wedding

1443. The restaurant shaped like an ocean liner on Route 22

1444. Paying fees at the university on my first day in Perugia

1445. Driving past the Sheraton Tara on the Mass Pike in the '80s

1446. Wearing lipstick to a restaurant in Burlington with Lucy and Knox Cummin

1447. Playing with my three little girls in a stream in Geneseo earlier this year, in August '99

1448. Listening to Noam Chomsky lecture at Harvard's Freshman Union

1449. Kids' rides at the Coney Island boardwalk in the last few years

1450. The dirt road to my sister Alice's house in West Virginia in the mid-'90s

1451. Talking with that Yugoslavian couple in Chamonix

1452. The wall around the private road near the Kalaidjians' house

1453. Crossing the scary street in Gloucester on that fatal day, April 26, 1986

1454. The hypermarket in Grenoble

1455. The main square in Vicenza during our honeymoon

1456. That party at Peter Kearny's on Scotland Rd. in 8th grade

1457. That bar near the archaeological museum in Siracusa

1458. The funicular in downtown Grenoble

1459. Patches of ice on the parking lot at the indoor tennis courts in West Orange

1460. Lynn Brodie's mother asking me about my brother John during the '69 strike at Harvard Law School

1461. Waiting for Sandy Stillman to pick me up in his Beetle at E.J. Korvette in the summer after high-school graduation

1462. Walking with Gary Lovesky past cannons embedded in concrete on Benefit St. in Providence

1463. Walking around MIT with Owen Andrews and the baby Charlotte

1464. Those obscure streets near Chuck Schwartz's house in Maplewood during high school

1465. Waiting for the train with Cynthia Zarin and Gino near Lake Trasimeno

1466. Throwing a football with Mark Woldin behind Mrs. Lang's house in the '80s

1467. Walking around the disappointing Lake Averno outside Naples during my year abroad

1468. Entering that big cemetery from the banks of the Seekonk River

1469. Getting into the old Mercedes in Louisa's grandmother's garage in Georgetown in '89

1470. Looking at Center City Philadelphia in the distance with Lucy Cummin in '92

1471. The mud room at Neal Besser's house in South Orange

1472. A dream about a bookstore on Wyoming Ave. in South Orange

1473. Pulling over to pick up a chunk of coal in the Lehigh Valley during our driving tour of the Northeast

1474. Getting lost with Owen Andrews on roads near Lowell

1475. Driving with Prudence Steiner to pick up Saga cheese at an upscale store in Cambridge

1476. The intersection of South Orange Ave. and Centre St. on a freezing day

1477. That seafood restaurant in Catania

1478. Driving through Shinnecock Hills golf course at night earlier this year, in July '99

1479. Peter Baker telling someone that I "didn't know one word of French" in Avignon

1480. Walking with Janet Murray through Mt. Lebanon Shaker village during my paternity leave

1481. Walking uphill with Dave Gurien to Meredith Kamen's house in Newstead during high school

1482. Stopping for gas on the Beltway during a drive to visit Owen Andrews in Virginia

1483. Steve Weis's living room

1484. A sumptuous scene from the movie "The Age of Innocence"

1485. A nine-year-old boy trying to steal money from Peter Baker and me at night on the Boylston St. bridge in Cambridge

1486. Eating with Kate Augenblick at the new snackbar at the Club in 8th grade

1487. Driving to Burlington airport with Lucy and Knox Cummin

1488. Lurking at night with Mark Woldin outside Roree Iris's house in 8th grade

1489. Walking on Grove Rd. past a house that burned during high school

1490. The glacier lake in Chamonix

1491. Louisa talking about a childhood friend's divorce in Battery Park City in the '90s

1492. Burnt trees along Route 27 in the Hamptons in the late '90s

1493. That peephole in the soaped window on Wall Street

1494. Sitting at the desk in my dorm room at Domaine Université in Grenoble

1495. Writing poetry in my room in an apartment building on the outskirts of Grenoble

1496. Walking up a path to a frozen waterfall in New Lebanon a week ago, on December 29, 1999

1497. A plaque about the Holocaust on a college dorm in Leiden during our big European trip

1498. Driving south on Charlton Ave. from Irving Ave. during a visit back to South Orange

1499. Watching "The March of the Wooden Soldiers" with my sister Liz during childhood

1500. Dreaming an armed man chased me around the Club in a Naples fleabag during my year abroad

1501. The sink in my room at Domaine Université

1502. Walking with Louisa in San Francisco in '92

1503. Alice Lichtenstein's reading at that place under the Brooklyn Bridge

1504. Dropping off Aunt Miriam's niece Tammy Benyami on the Upper West Side after a Passover in the late '80s

1505. That corn plot near the tennis courts in Grenoble

1506. Walking around MIT with Owen Andrews

1507. Driving toward massive Mt. Katadyn during trip season at Kennebec senior

1508. Picnicking with Uncle Milton and Aunt Miriam during our boat trip

1509. My brother Sandy pointing out Ralph Boynton's old cycle shop in Cambridge during college

1510. Walking along the wall of the factory to Mac Gander's apartment on Leland St.

1511. The view of Central Park from our room in Essex House on our 10th anniversary in '99

1512. Louisa telling me about a time her cousin Cabell Bruce failed to show up in the '80s

1513. Looking at the impressive Maplewood municipal building

1514. Leaving the archaeological museum in Siracusa

1515. Watching kids sled in backyards at my brother Sandy's house in Milton

1516. The thrift shop in Bethpage

1517. Burnt scrub pines on Route 27

1518. Walking by the huge Quick house on Montrose Ave. during junior high

1519. That frigid day with Peter Baker, Gary Lovesky and Manya Daner along the Seekonk River

1520. Drinking sangria by the fountain of Arethusa in Siracusa

1521. Mitchell Price's front door in Maplewood during high school

1522. The rhododendrons outside the 4th grade entrance to Marshall School

1523. The Italian 20th century collection in Milan during our honeymoon

1524. Looking through a bus window at the caves under Perugia

1525. Driving past a little restaurant on Noyack Rd. in the Hamptons in the '90s

1526. Driving past Ethical Culture in Maplewood during high school

1527. Hearing about the Shah's death with Cynthia Zarin in Annecy

1528. The paddle tennis court in John Elson's backyard in L.A. in '96

1529. An Italian guy who liked Bob Dylan in Perugia

1530. That seafood restaurant in Catania

1531. Walking along the river behind Oxford colleges during my trip to Britain

1532. Staying at a B&B near a nursing home in New Boston, Mass., during our driving tour of the Northeast

1533. Sitting with Louisa on a stone wall in Manchester

1534. Driving from Livingston Mall to the Club on Eisenhower Parkway during a college vacation

1535. The carwash near Mac Gander's apartment on Ibbotson St. in Somerville

1536. Leaving the ducal palace in Urbino with Cynthia Zarin and Nancy Sinkoff during my year abroad

1537. Driving with Louisa and our three little girls on a side road to avoid Jersey Turnpike holiday traffic

1538. Walking with French vocabulary cards in my back pocket in Charlestown in '81

1539. Walking past the Kessler house on shady Charlton Ave.

1540. Playing tennis "like McEnroe" at Larry Travis's club in L.A. in the late '70s

1541. Playing softball in Steve Kurens' big side yard

1542. Looking toward the B'nai Israel parking lot from Andy Freundlich's house in 7th grade

1543. Stopping for a chocolate donut after a day as a sub at East Boston High

1544. Eating at a pizzeria in New Lebanon during my paternity leave

1545. The hiding place where Sharon Mastrangelo and I made out in 8th grade

1546. Walking past Ginger Meehan's house on Ralston Ave. during junior high

1547. Walking around Tufts with Lili Porten in '99

1548. Playing stickball with Mark Woldin at Marshall School during a college vacation

1549. Driving through New Brunswick on the way to Billy and Molly Wood's house in '99

1550. A traffic light in the middle of nowhere on Route 17 during a drive to Geneseo in the late '90s

1551. Sneaking into a partly burned mansion on Centre St. near the VA hospital in 4th grade

1552. Waiting for Ben Blackmer at that Cincinnati recording studio

1553. CHS tennis coach Vic Lomakin at the South Orange courts

1554. Looking at oysterweed in the parking lot of the Bethpage printing plant

1555. Picking corn that time near the tennis courts in Grenoble

1556. Watching a punted football pass in and out of the sunlight at Grove Park in the summer after college graduation

1557. Taking mushrooms with Mark Woldin at Mrs. Lang's house during graduate school

1558. Teeing off at dusk with Andy Fried on the 9th hole at the Club during a college vacation

1559. Seeing the white clover from Deena Shoshkes and Jon Fried's car

1560. Watching trains with Owen Andrews on that boiling day in Roanoke

1561. Abby Weinberg's house on Montrose Ave. in the fall after college graduation

1562. The parking lot around the South Orange tennis courts

1563. The Old Stone Bank in downtown Providence during graduate school

1564. Prudence Steiner's section of Cambridge near Mt. Auburn Cemetery

1565. Frantically crossing the Champs-Élysées with Milton Longe during my year abroad

1566. The bridge over the stream near the Nations Farm in Geneseo in the late '90s

1567. Talking about Osip Mandelstam with Professor Al Cook outside Rockefeller Library at Brown

1568. Walking away from the outdoor bus station in Perugia

1569. Reading John Wesley Powell's The Exploration of the Colorado River during my cross-country trip

1570. Watching Mr. Duckett play basketball at the South Orange community center during high school

1571. Waiting for Ben Blackmer at that Cincinnati recording studio

1572. Watching workers silver-paint a roof near the East Hampton train station in the mid-'90s

1573. The parking lot at Pal's Cabin during the last years of Dad's life

1574. Abandoned mansions with stained-glass windows on Centre St. in 4th grade

1575. That seafood restaurant in Catania

1576. Walking down the steep street to my first apartment in Perugia

1577. Hanging out with Ned Patz and Jerry Gordon at the Camp Takajo tennis invitation

1578. The big public parking lot behind the A&P in East Hampton

1579. Smoking a cigarette with Frank Stecker by the brook behind SOJH

1580. Scoping out a high-end hifi store in New Brunswick for Tech Hifi

1581. Talking to Suki Ryan at Jon Fried's bowling party in '87

1582. Rhoda Metzger and Glenn Ruga announcing they were going out at her birthday party in 6th grade

1583. Walking west on Montrose Ave. from Steve Kurens' house

1584. Driving from my brother Sandy's house in Charlestown to Lili Porten's apartment in Cambridge a few months ago, in September 2000

1585. That frigid day with Peter Baker, Gary Lovesky and Manya Daner along the Seekonk River

1586. The Bessers' kitchen in South Orange

1587. Playing tennis with Steve Riegel in Maplewood during a college summer vacation

1588. Visiting Steve Kurens' house with Mac Gander after college graduation

1589. Beth Duddy and Philip Mosenthal's living room in Harriman

1590. Looking at Newtown Creek in Brooklyn's Greenpoint during my New York walks

1591. That doctor's office on South Orange Ave. near Joe Zente's house

1592. The temple with steep steps at Ostia Antica during our big European trip

1593. Standing outside Peter Goldman's house in Newstead at night in 9th grade

1594. The front of Alice Lichtenstein's house in Oneonta, N.Y., during my paternity leave

1595. Driving past Nancy Enzminger's house on Ridgewood Rd. in the '70s

1596. Walking downhill from Tufts to a coffeehouse in the summer after 11th grade

1597. Buying Mexican food with my nephew Dave Travis at a drive-in in L.A. in '96

1598. That obscure street behind Steve Longo's house

1599. Walking by the Quicks' huge house on Montrose Ave.

1600. Sitting in the park near the Educational Alliance

1601. The face of Suki Ryan in the '80s

1602. Driving with Owen Andrews past a soft ice cream place in West Virginia in the mid-'80s

1603. Hiking with Neal Besser down from Sunfish Pond that chaotic night in 9th grade

1604. Playing wiffle ball with Uncle Sam Rich near a lake on a fall day during early childhood

1605. Walking west up Irving Ave. past Dr. Kohn's house

1606. Dinner at a Pennsylvania inn with Bill Wood, Louisa and a crying Charlotte two weeks after her birth

1607. The trestle over the train tracks at Mountain Station in 9th grade

1608. Driving on Vauxhall Rd. in Millburn toward Route 22

1609. The pizza place in New Lebanon during my paternity leave

1610. Talking to Gordon Boggie in Cliff Greenberg's backyard in 5th grade

1611. Those mushrooms at Steve Weis's house

1612. Louisa's family's house in Manchester

1613. Driving past Ann's Clam Bar in West Orange

1614. A country store near Bill Wood's farm in the late '80s

1615. Lunching at Uncle Milton's house in Westhampton

1616. The Quicks' huge house on Montrose Ave. during junior high

1617. Playing a tennis match at Camp Takajo on a 103 degree day

1618. Plagued by a cardboard box caught on our tire as we drove away from Boston in '99

1619. The house on Montrose Ave. where an orphan named Grant spent the summer after 3rd grade

1620. Driving with Owen Andrews and Nancy Hurrelbrinck into Ocean Grove, joking about "God slicking back his hair"

1621. Shael Brachman's wedding party near the Boston Arboretum last year, in September '00

1622. Taking the ferry from Orient Point to New London, Conn., in August '00

1623. That dinner at a Pennsylvania inn with Bill Wood, Louisa and the newborn Charlotte

1624. Taking a bus from one Milan airport to another after my trip to Sicily

1625. The shady apple tree by the pool at Bill Wood's farm during the last years of his life

1626. Talking to those Yugoslavians in Chamonix

1627. Watching Mr. Duckett play basketball at the South Orange community center

1628. Crossing the scary street to the seafood restaurant in Gloucester on that fatal day, April 26, 1986

DREAMS
OF THE 1990s

the morning of Monday, September 22, 1991

My wife, Louisa, and I were riding home in Brooklyn on a baby elephant. We reached a section of Flatbush Ave. that was under construction. One lane was closed off. We had to jump down from the elephant, which promptly ran away and disappeared. Louisa was sure the elephant would be fine. We continued home on foot. During a particularly drab stretch of 4th Ave., we stopped to look inside an industrial hangar. Back outside, I noticed the elephant heading toward us. Something was wrong. The elephant turned around. Its left hindleg had been bashed in by a car. Distraught, I wondered if the elephant had to be shot like a horse, or if the leg could heal.

the morning of Saturday, October 5, 1991

Louisa and I were staying at one of those old luxury hotels. We were involved in a plot with my friend Gary Lovesky and some goons to burn the place down. In the early afternoon, we checked out and met Gary in the jungle nearby. He instructed us to wait there, without showing our faces, until he returned from torching the hotel. We wandered around the bizarre terrain—a huge overgrown crater in front of the hotel, rimmed on all sides by highways. I suddenly had to pee. I don't know why, but I never thought of going in the jungle. After a tense discussion, Louisa and I decided to return to the hotel. It was large enough for us to use another entrance, so we wouldn't be recognized. I moved stealthily toward a bathroom a few steps above the lobby. An icy woman barred the way. She refused to let me pass, even after I protested that I had stayed there the previous night. As we left, I thought, "They deserve to get burned down. It serves them right." The next thing I knew, we were walking around an outdoor mall, looking in the boutique windows. I picked up several brochures in the shops and stowed them in my bookbag. Then we went to the ballet. One of the ballerinas, who was sitting several rows behind us, took my bag to borrow a brush or mirror. She left it at her seat, which bothered me, because I might not be able to retrieve it after the performance, and it contained incriminating evidence. When the show began, it turned out our seats were cramped against the right side of the stage. We decided to leave. Outside, I realized I didn't have my bag. Maybe it didn't matter: There were only brochures inside, no personal documents. Standing there on an outside staircase, high above a bridge and a river, we noticed the sky was a peculiar color, a smoky purple. The sunset? No. It was a huge column of smoke blowing across the sky. It had to be from the hotel. We just walked along, trying to be relaxed, though we checked a TV somewhere to see if we had been implicated.

the morning of Wednesday, October 9, 1991

I was packing up my childhood home in South Orange to move out after the death of my brother David in 1972. I packed all day and night. I thought I had taken care of everything. But I realized there was a lot to do in one room upstairs. In another room upstairs, too. The most important rooms. My rooms. How would I get everything done?

the morning of Thursday, October 24, 1991

We were moving into a new apartment on the top floor of a much wider building. I unloaded a truck in front with the contractor Mike Streaman, who renovated our apartment last year. Someone said there was a fire in the building. I looked at the top-floor windows. At first, I discerned nothing, but then I noticed a faint charring. Upstairs, we walked through the apartment, a large unfinished room that was somewhat dark. I looked around and wondered where the other rooms were. It was supposed to be a large apartment. Why were we moving here, anyway? Louisa was removing glasses from the drainboard and packing them to go downstairs, so they wouldn't be destroyed by fire. I said they'd been left by a previous tenant, we needed to repack what we'd just brought up. Streaman tapped my shoulder and pointed to a door into another wing. "That's where the fire is," he said, "do you want to take a look at it?" "No!" I had no interest in seeing the fire. Instead, I immediately started repacking books and manuscripts.

the morning of Thursday, November 7, 1991

I was sitting at a card table with a group of old ladies and Grandma Fenton, my dead step-grandmother, the mother of my father's first wife. Thrilled by the once-in-a-lifetime opportunity, I asked Grandma Fenton what it was like to be dead. She frowned and said she usually didn't exist at all. That was especially so at the beginning, when she was first dead. I remembered she had been a smoker and tried to guess what brand she smoked. "Marlboro Lights" popped into my head (though they didn't exist when Grandma Fenton was alive). I was pleasantly surprised that I remembered her brand after all these years. A few seconds later, she pulled out a bright cigarette box. The next thing I knew, I was driving with my mother and my sister Liz to Grandma Fenton's beach club, which was located on the Jersey shore near New York City now, not near Asbury Park. Mom muttered something about the water being so polluted that you could burn your skin. Liz and I were looking forward to seeing one of the employees, whom we remembered from childhood. It wasn't the man at the front desk, but the black bartender.

the morning of Saturday, November 30, 1991

A bunch of people, including a group of six woman, paid a weekend visit to my childhood friend Steve Kurens' house, which was perched on a hillside. We watched a lot of basketball on TV. At the end of the weekend, I warned Steve that the women were going to rob the rest of us. He didn't pay much heed. A minute later, I stepped outside. Sure enough, I saw the women running away with the loot. I also noticed a big fire up in the hills. I left, hiking up a steep overgrown road to the shed where I had parked my car. The shed was full of people, including several bums drinking and partying inside my car! The paint job and the interior of the car were ruined. I started making threats, but no one responded. "Will someone give me a ride to the police?" I asked. "I will," a man said, but he kept fiddling around, not making a move to help me. I stormed off and quickly found a park visitors' office, where there were several policemen. When I told them what had happened, they started listing reasons why no insurer would cover it. They said a state law had been passed to the effect that the shed was no longer on park property. Also, they said there were NO PARKING signs on the shed, though I hadn't seen any.

the morning of Thursday, December 5, 1991

My friend Lucy Cummin persuaded me to climb a mountain. The hike began inside an ethnographic museum. In the stairway up from the basement, I paused to look at carved wooden sticks mounted on the wall. Behind thin vertical glass panels, objects were embedded in the earth outside the building's foundation. When I reached the top of the stairs, I saw a poppy waving in the wind and thought, "Oh, I'll be seeing poppies again." I tried to think what else went with poppies. We sat on the grass for a few minutes until Lucy wanted to push onward. I told her I was worried I would be cold at the higher altitudes. She said, "Just pull the parka out of your pack if you need it." I held up my pack, which was very light. I had forgotten the parka. I had forgotten everything I needed. Lucy criticized me. I said, "If you hadn't decided to go on the spur of the moment and hurried me so, I wouldn't have forgotten it."

the morning of Monday, December 10, 1991

At a banquet with my dead father, I was disturbed to see my college friend Mac Gander at a nearby table. Afterward, I was driving Dad back to our hotel down a broad and brightly lit avenue. I must have missed a turn, because I reached a river and then wound up on an expressway heading north out of town. A Clark bar materialized out of nowhere in my right hand, making it hard to grasp the steering wheel. I got off at the first exit and stopped at a country gas station, where I tried to push the Clark bar back into a candy machine, without success.

the morning of Friday, December 13, 1991

I was standing with a couple of others near an antique car in a large garage. It occurred to me that in the loft upstairs, there might be some books about Louisa's late grandmother, Maude Hunnewell Atherton, whom we called Dally. At this point, I became Dally. Attending a girls' school in rural England in the beginning of the 20th century, I was in love with a race car driver who visited me from time to time. Then I heard he had been killed in an accident. At the end, I was playing croquet on a huge field with clumps of trees, tall grass and hummocks. It was very difficult.

82

the morning of Thursday, December 26, 1991

I was riding with my great-uncle Leslie Handler on the subway. At a stop, he got off and I stayed on. Sitting there, I remembered Uncle Leslie died this year. I tried to get off the subway to tell him, but the doors closed on me.

✳

Louisa and I were walking up the monumental steps of a university library. I noticed a very tall man sleeping on the steps under a blanket. I made a comment about it, and she said he was one of her art-history professors.

the afternoon of Monday, January 6, 1992

In a narrow storefront, I was sitting on a couch next to a guy my age. I recognized him, but couldn't remember his name. Greg Faro, the legendary "Greek" from junior high? No, it was someone I'd known much later than that. Then Mark Miller—from my college days hanging out with Doc Humes—walked into the store. He was wearing a hat shaped like a pyramid. A new person was sitting next to me on the couch now, a heavy guy with stringy hair. At first, I didn't recognize him in the poor lighting, but then I realized it was my college friend John Phillips, who also hung out with Doc. I told him how happy I was to see him. At that point, an armored personnel carrier drove past us down South Orange Ave. One of the people in the storefront said we didn't need to worry about it. It wouldn't bother us before the evening. Fearing it would turn around at South Orange station, I hurried out of the store.

the morning of Friday, January 10, 1992

I was visiting a house that had supposedly been in my friend Sandy Stillman's family for many years. A very old man walked past with a German novel that pricked my interest. He disappeared through one of those low, triangular attic doorways. Who was he? Mrs. Stillman said he had been living there since Kafka's time. He wasn't any trouble at all. He didn't even need food. There was an old woman in the house, too. Later, I decided to go into the old man's room to find the book. A loose weave of leather strips partially obstructed the doorway. I was worried the man would be there, but he wasn't. The room

83

was surprisingly small, with only enough room for a cot and a table by a gray window. There were no books, or anything else for that matter, except for a clock radio on the table frozen at 12:15. I sat down and picked up a doll with long red hair. Its arms accidentally brushed the sides of my penis.

the morning of Wednesday, January 15, 1992

Vacationing up north with my friend Owen Andrews and his fiancé, Eleanor Tittmann, we drove to the coast one day. The place was wrecked by big earth movers. I suggested we enter a walled Maine town nearby, which looked cute, and get something to eat, even though we had eaten not long before. Owen, Eleanor and Louisa wandered into a house. I tagged along, but stopped in the mud room, where I prepared a bowl of yogurt. When I realized there were people in the house, I worried I would get in trouble for helping myself. I stepped into the kitchen and met the three women who lived there, two of whom were widows. The main one said, "I bet you're from New Jersey." "How did you know that? My accent?" She nodded. We talked around the dining-room table until the ghosts of their husbands appeared and the four of us fled. Later, at the end of our trip, Louisa and I were trying to figure out what was left to do. There was a bird sanctuary that we hadn't visited on an island just off the tip of a peninsula. We looked at it across the water. It was small and round, not very exciting. There were rangers all around it, with crazy birds flying toward them. I noticed the water below was roiled by fish. Maybe the birds were hunting the fish, which were trying to get away. They leapt over a wall onto the tip of peninsula and slithered across the ground to a fountain. I tried to catch one, finally grabbing a small fish, which I decided was big enough for dinner. "Should I clean it now?" I asked Louisa. "No, it'll keep better if you don't," she said. I wrapped it in plastic and put it in my new jacket, but there was a problem with the drawstrings. "That's what happens when somebody buys everyone the same Christmas present," I said. "Usually, it isn't very good." Finally, I got the cheap drawstrings to work.

I was talking on the phone to Owen, who was visiting New York. Then I walked down a narrow hallway, which had many more dark antiques than it used to have. Inside a palatial hall, I had a talk with Teddy Roosevelt, who was complaining the public had rejected him. Hadn't he been in office his entire life, I asked. All true, but he wasn't being sent to the Senate. He said our state had a male and a female senator, one of whom was too liberal, the other too conservative. Later, I heard that the male senator, who had become a basketball player, was being traded to a Canadian team, opening up a spot for Teddy. At the end, I got to see Owen. We were walking to a train station, accompanied by a couple with two children. The kids were romping in the shady suburban street, holding us up. Suddenly, it was 3:10, only twenty minutes before departure. The station was at the bottom of a big hill, within reach if we picked up the pace. The couple decided we should race ahead, they weren't going to make the train. It struck me as odd that people would just decide to abandon their plans like that. At the station, really just a crossing, we kept looking down the tracks for the train, but it didn't come. More people showed up, including Owen's brother John. A pot pipe was passed around. Right then, someone said the train was coming. A loud whistle blew. As the train pulled up, I noticed a bunch of things from my bag were strewn on the ground, mainly toiletries. Spastic, I had a hard time gathering them together. The conductor grew impatient. "I'm hurrying," I said, "but my hand's frozen." The train started moving as I was sweeping up the last thing, the broken electric razor that Dad bought me not long before he died. In terror, I thought, "What will happen if I lose it?" I don't know whether I saved it or not. On the train, which was much wider and higher than any normal train, I dropped my stuff on a seat, and realized I might have left the outside door open. I went back to the steps. The door seemed to be ajar, swinging slightly. Should I shut it? Before I had the chance, a woman from the floor below shut it, giving me a critical glance. Back above, in the aisle, I noticed three big ships out the window, lit up at night. "The train's running along a wide river," I thought. Maybe I should switch my seat to that side and write something? Instead, I walked up the aisle, vaguely looking for a bathroom. I had trouble reading the signs. Then I saw LADIES, GENTLEMEN, but they didn't lead to bathrooms. They led to amusement-park booths. People were throwing beanbags onto a pile of hoops, trying to get the hoops to pop into the air and land around stuffed animals. I decided to try. But I couldn't get free of the crowd to make a good throw. People kept brushing against my back. Finally, I got one off, not bad. As I was leaving, in search of a bathroom again, my boss at *The Wall Street Journal*, Marty Schenker, walked in. I told him to watch out for people interfering with his throw from behind.

the morning of Wednesday, March 4, 1992

Driving around a suburb in Argentina, lost, we pulled over to consult a road map. Streets and rivers seemed interchangeable. We tried to figure out which rivers ran together, so we could get to the heart of Buenos Aires. Later, we parked outside an ancient house and looked in a window at an aristocratic bedroom. The house's furniture and decor reminded me of the Elizabethans. We sat down at a table and were served authentic pancakes by a guide dressed in period costume. A man with us flung a bill on the table as we left, which seemed totally unnecessary to me—and even a little insulting. The guide stared at it for a second and snapped it up. "Everyone needs money," the man said.

the morning of Saturday, March 14, 1992

We were staying at a primitive house in the woods. Standing at an upstairs window, I noticed three animals below in the clearing, two small ones and a large one. I pulled out a rifle and gathered it would be alright to shoot them through the glass. Later, on the front steps, we talked with a boy who was holding two dead furry animals. He pointed to a bullet wound in his chest. Was he the large animal? I couldn't believe it. I hadn't shot a boy. I'd shot a bear. My father-in-law, the estate lawyer William P. Wood, told the boy to have his lawyer contact Michael Ruby, spelling out my name for him.

My *Journal* friend Tom Walker told me about a woman reporter he didn't like. Shortly afterward, she pulled me aside and started describing a plan to place thousands of African-American children for adoption in Florida. She whipped out a map of the state and pointed to a rural district, illustrating all the economic problems of sending more poor people there. She asked me to call the governor of Nevada to persuade him to take 5,000 kids there. This made me nervous—and didn't sound very promising. "Don't you think I should write instead?" "No, you should call." "The governor himself? Isn't he busy?" "No, he's a good guy." The thought passed through my mind that Nevada had become more liberal in recent years. "Should I tell him I'm with the *Journal*?" "Yes, definitely." As the reporter and I started to drift apart, she said, "Normally, I talk like this, but sometimes I talk in a way that you don't understand." Her voice changed to that of a Southern sharecropper. I said, "Oh, I can understand that if I make the effort. My father grew up under the worst Jim Crow in Tulsa." I wandered away, crossing a twilit lawn to a wedding tent, where people were being served dinner. When the waitress came around, I asked to be served, but she didn't serve me. She served everyone else around me, even those who came in later. Finally, I blew up. Everyone was shocked. Did I get too mad? Afterward, she slid a plate in front of me. It didn't have potato pancakes, the thing I was looking forward to most, but that didn't surprise me.

the morning of Monday, March 23, 1992

A guy turned a drawing of mine into a painting. I was shocked to find the painting had someone else's signature. The guy tried to convince me such changes were inevitable. I took many steps, including legal ones, to get the signature changed.

✳

I was taking a walk with my *Journal* friend Ezra Palmer. Discussing where we were, he said we were in Manhattan's Inwood, and I maintained we were east of Audubon Ave. Then I realized we were in the streets near the VA hospital in East Orange. Ezra wandered off. I went looking for him, calling his name down each block. Some neighborhood kids picked up the chant, creating an echo effect that I didn't find very pleasing. I passed the beginning of 4th Ave. and 2nd Ave., right next to each other, like some of those streets in the West Village. I concluded I was definitely in Brooklyn. I passed mansions being completely renovated and turned into businesses, as in Edinburgh. Two had signs that began CONSENSUAL. I reached 9th St. and thought to myself, "This won't lead to the Botanic Garden." I found Ezra at that point. We looked at a map that showed that 9th St. did indeed lead to the garden. On the way, we passed two black boys. The smaller boy, hiding behind the other's legs, poked his head out. He was smoking a cigar!

the morning of Tuesday, March 24, 1992

Standing outside Mac Gander's cottage, I talked with two girls, who I assumed were his daughters. Mac took me inside to a small back room, which had beautiful mahogany furniture, mirrors and girandoles, but was too symmetrical for my taste. In a front room, he suddenly said to me, "This is a real failure." "What?" I asked, unsure if I had heard him correctly. "A failure." "What's a failure? That we're seeing each other?" He nodded. "I don't know," I said, "I was passing by and thought it couldn't hurt. ... Do you know the last time we saw each other?" "In April of '82," he said. I smiled at his error. "No, it was June, late June of '83, at a Japanese restaurant with you and Emily. Don't you remember?" Mac started to get angry. "I'm sick of hearing talk like 'I was just passing through.' And what did you used to say? 'We're like two sisters.'" "I think we are," I broke in. "I'm no one's sister," he shouted, and shoved me out of the house.

the morning of Wednesday, March 25, 1992

I dreamt I was driving an old yellow schoolbus. It stalled near a big park and the pneumatic door sprang open. A hard guy standing outside the door said, "Don't even try to restart the bus and get away." I made a quick try. He jumped in and said, "Get out, NOW!" I walked away, giving up on the bus altogether, until I realized that maybe I could buy it back from him. What was he going to do with an old schoolbus? I yelled out, "Can I buy it back for $100?" "$100? It isn't even worth that. $40 or $30." I started walking back toward him, but he walked away from the bus. "Maybe I'll get it back for free," I thought. Right then, a group of younger guys came up to me. One demanded that I pay him the $30. I pulled out my bills. The top one was a hundred. The kid grabbed it. The one beneath also was a hundred. Shit! "Give us that one, too," the kid said. "I need to pay someone off," I blurted out. They could understand that. As I hurried to the bus, I congratulated myself on saving the second hundred. At home, I told Louisa and her father about my dream. Midway, they stopped listening and started talking about something else. "Listen," I broke in, "this is the good part."

the morning of Tuesday, April 7, 1992

I was driving somewhere and missed my turn, which didn't overly concern me. After passing a raised reservoir, I reached a dead end and parked. I walked down a long flight of stairs to a small city with more Catholic churches than I've ever seen. It was such a beautiful place, such a beautiful day. It had rained earlier, and now the sun was breaking through. Steam was rising on the empty playgrounds. Eventually, I reached a hotel set into the hillside. Maybe I could get back to my car by going through the hotel? Inside, I tried to be unobtrusive, but a woman noticed me and came on to me. Then a man buttonholed me. He wanted to know how expensive something was that cost two or three million lire. After slowly calculating, I said, "It's about $2,000."

I waited for a long time outside the office of a black teacher at my old high school. When we finally started to talk, the bell rang, ending the period. Accompanying him in the hall, I asked him something stupid like "Why do so few eligible black students go to law school?" He seemed to realize that I wasn't the average student, that I could be a teacher. After we split up, I walked through the halls on my own, trying to decide which class I wanted to attend. I looked in Mr. Stickel's classroom. There he was, with only three or four math students in the room, all seated near his desk, which didn't surprise me. I passed Mr. Palma's physics class. I assumed the next room would be chemistry, but couldn't remember my teacher's name, probably for embarrassing sexual reasons. "Chemistry's definitely something I need to learn," I thought to myself. "What else do I need to learn? That's what I need to figure out. Pick four or five subjects and take those." At the end of the hall, I was surprised to see a coffee bar. I decided to stop there. At the counter, as I was about to order, a burly guy pushed up. "Three to go," he said. "Wait a minute," I said meekly. The counterwoman heeded me. "One coffee," I said. "Well, if it isn't Michael Ruby," she said. "Do you know who I am?" Her face enlarged in front of my eyes. "Cheryl Dunsker," I said. I wondered how my vivacious 10th grade girlfriend had ended up there.

In Pittsburgh's Greyhound terminal, I was waiting for a bus to Chicago. There was an announcement over the loudspeakers that a bomb had exploded on one of the bridges out of the city, causing a delay. It wasn't known how long it would last. Later, I rode on a bus through old Midwestern suburbs, but without many trees. It was very bright and hot out. I was sitting in the front seat, next to a small young woman with curly hair. "I wonder if I could make it with her," I thought, "I could have fun with a girl like that." She mentioned she was from Middleburg, Virginia. "I've been there a number of times," I said. She said, "It seems like you've been a lot of places. I've mainly been there and New Jersey." "I grew up in New Jersey!" I said. We nestled against each other.

the morning of Tuesday, April 21, 1992

I was standing on a riverbank, looking at an island not far away. I wanted to swim to it. But there was an underwater net that stretched across the channel. A woman warned me not to get swept into the net and drown. That's what happened to a lot of runaway slaves, she said. I said the current didn't look very strong. On the island, there was a large deserted house. I went inside to find a piece of cloth to stanch the blood flowing from a wound between my right thumb and forefinger. Through the window, I noticed a group of college girls in white dresses coming up to the house for a picnic. When they saw me, I called out that they shouldn't worry, I was leaving shortly. But they ran away. A few minutes later, a troop of policemen approached, like the federales at the end of John Huston's "Treasure of the Sierra Madre." What should I do? I opened the door to the basement and started descending. There were thick cobwebs across the steps. I reached for something to sweep them away. At the bottom, I got caught in more cobwebs. I noticed a door with a shiny new lock, which surprised me. It led outside. I started walking away from the house, up a path into the woods. A cop came around the house to that door. I was so near him I had to freeze and hope he didn't see me. He didn't. I walked away. After a minute, a heavy black cop saw me. I ran like crazy through woods and then across fields, but I couldn't shake him. How could a fat guy run so fast? Each time I looked behind me, he was much closer than he ought to be, taking aim with his gun. I would start zigzagging, though I didn't expect that to save me. For some reason, he never fired.

the morning of Tuesday, July 7, 1992

Louisa and I went out to dinner. Sometime during the meal, one of us started worrying about getting robbed. As we were leaving, I noticed a group of photos leaning against the flower in the middle of the table. They were very bright photos of me, some with Mom, from my teens in South Orange. When we returned to our building, which had a retail establishment on the ground floor, Louisa wanted to ask someone to come up with us, in case there was a robber. I balked at the idea. We argued. I went up myself, but didn't proceed any farther than the first room of the apartment, which hadn't been disturbed. Suddenly very tired, I lay down and dozed. When Louisa came up, we argued again.

Then, I went through the French doors to look at the rest of the apartment. In the dim rooms, I saw boxes on the floor, pictures taken down from walls. Without actually noticing anything missing, I said, "I guess that's the end of the silver."

the morning of Friday, July 10, 1992

I was at my college girlfriend Cynthia Zarin's house. She was saying, "Don't I look great?" as she modeled clothes. She did look great. "I've been buying a lot of clothes lately," she said. The remark struck me as odd. Did it have a secret meaning? Like when I had said to her earlier, "Of course, someone could accept five or ten of my poems at once and that would change everything." A friend of Cynthia's showed up. The friend had been touted as beautiful, but I found her unbearable. Cynthia hinted that she and her husband, Mike, had broken up. He was coming by to pick up his dog, which was upstairs. I had to go outside to move my car to another parking place. Once I started driving, I didn't see any spaces. I couldn't turn around either. I was getting farther away from Cynthia's. I got tangled up with the off ramp of a highway. Oh well, I didn't really want to go back.

the morning of Thursday, July 16, 1992

I was home in South Orange on vacation from college. The living room didn't open into the recessed second living room anymore. There was a wall where the two steps down had been, with a raw picture window in the middle of the wall. Probably the rooms on the second and third stories over the second living room also didn't exist anymore. That really got me. I had stuff up there. Now it was lost. The picture window looked out on shit, a gravel alley. The living room was cramped, too. Forever cramped. "Why did you make it so small?" I asked my sister Liz. No answer. "Did you do it because the contractor talked you into putting in the window while he was doing the other work on the house?" I detected a nod. Furious, I screamed, "Why couldn't you talk to me about it before you did it?" I grabbed the pillow she was holding and tore it to shreds. There were feathers all over the floor. I stormed off to the beach, where I met Owen and Tom Walker, who, for some reason, wanted to see a book about Theodore Gericault. I wasn't sure if I still had it.

92

the morning of Wednesday, July 29, 1992

During a drive in Manhattan, I was reading an article by a guy named Hudson about the fact that more than 100 people a day were disappearing in the New York subways, the first time that had happened since the 19th century. Back then, when the complaints mounted, the city rounded up people and forced them to clean up the subway. Something like that might happen again. I couldn't understand why a guy named Hudson would be writing about New York. Wasn't his family one of the founders of the famously corrupt Hudson County in New Jersey? But then it occurred to me that maybe he had something to do with Hudson St., where my sister Kathy lived until recently. After I finished the article, we drove across a bridge that supposedly connected Lower Manhattan to New Jersey. I saw a very strange sight—people outside in the midst of the traffic. They were on rollerblades or skateboards, towed by cars. "I'd feel so exposed," I said to Owen, who was driving. "I already feel very exposed in a car," he said. Back in New Jersey, at a house like the Howards' in South Orange with a red-clay tennis court, there was a question about who was going to drive me back to Upper Manhattan. I went to the caretaker's cottage at the back of the property to pick up my tennis racquet, but there was a vicious dog inside.

the morning of Wednesday, September 30, 1992, in Antwerpen

In the hallway of a law office, I was looking for my great-uncle Milton Handler. I found him uncharacteristically asleep in his chair. Backing away, I bumped into his secretary, Eileen, but I wasn't sure what message to leave for the "professor." Later, Uncle Milton was sitting on a bench, talking to someone. "Well, actually," he said, "I've just been learning some important things from my dead father in a dream." My ears pricked up. "My father was a fine man and a patriot," he said as a little prologue, then told how his father believed the secret government of this country started with the murder of William Henry Harrison.

the morning of Sunday, October 4, 1992, in Amsterdam

Owen and I took a walk. He wanted to go in a direction that I said would cause us to miss the sunset. We went his way, and sure enough, we did miss the sunset, a spectacular one.

✽

The outgoing copy chief at the *Journal*, Rich Holden, took me into his office and began criticizing my work. He opened up a scrapbook filled with stories I had edited. I had no idea he had such a thing. It was a sickening feeling. He pointed to a paragraph in the hurricane story, then to the headline of a story dated April 41, a date that didn't cause me to bat an eyelash. Later, I was told to report to a certain room. I was apprehensive, but it turned out to be an auditorium. Rich's yet-to-be-named successor was there, a patch of hair missing on his head. He introduced me to the people in the audience.

✽

Liz was anxious for us to get to the train station. Inside the train, I suddenly became confused by a sticker on my ticket and stepped back onto the platform, leaving my luggage behind. I watched helplessly as the glass doors slid shut and the train pulled away. Speaking Italian with several people, I tried to figure out how to track down my luggage. Later, on the way to work, worrying about the phone inquiries I needed to make for the luggage, I also started to worry about a story on baseball I had uncharacteristically dropped the night before, its headline half-finished. I bumped into a colleague at the cashier's window on the top floor of a decaying office building. She said the assistant managing editor wanted to see me. I tried to think up an excuse. Of course, the luggage! But wait, I dropped the story half a day before I lost the luggage. "Don't worry about it," Ezra put in, "that new zero in L.A. wrote it, we quashed it, but then, after you left, the M.E. wanted it."

the morning of Tuesday, October 13, 1992, in Stockholm

I left my stale 35th birthday party in Brooklyn to take a stroll to my childhood home, where I did a few chores. I wondered if I was absenting myself from the party for too long. As I was leaving, a portiere of blankets in the front doorway fell down. I had a hard time fixing them. Right then, Louisa arrived. The phone rang. She picked it up, even though I didn't want her to. I wanted to leave. It was a drug dealer, supposedly a friend of Cynthia. He was trying to set up a Christmas party in a couple of days. In a hurry, I asked for his phone number, so I could get back to him. He wouldn't give it to me. His last name? Nope. "I don't see how I can possibly get in touch with you then," I said, irritated, looking for approval from Louisa, who was standing at the door the whole time. We worked out something or other. Later, Louisa and I were walking by a dock. I noticed a huge powerboat that belonged to the guy. "I don't know if I should be getting involved with people like this," I thought, "but it would be fun to ride in that boat."

the morning of Wednesday, November 4, 1992, in Wien

Once again, I was walking around a city looking for the Jewish section. Dad joined me at a restaurant. When he opened the menu, he said, "I won't eat pizza." "Don't worry, there's salad, too." Later, alone, I noticed a group of blonde women in frilly pink skirts walking around an overweight man, who was seated in a chair writing. I heard they were "facilitators for the Queen," and he was a novelist who followed the Queen from place to place. I wondered how he managed to write so much in such conditions. Continuing with my tourist's day, I walked uphill to the church with the statue of the infant Jesus that cries real tears. Crude wooden bleachers had been erected around the shrine. I started to take a seat in the middle, but then noticed one in front on the right, near a large group of seven-year-olds. One of their teachers said something rude to me. Later, I was riding in a crowded car through a flat, gray landscape. A woman in the backseat said she couldn't believe that people kept living here among 40-year-old ruins without fixing them up. I said there were places in Sicily, such as Siracusa, where people had been living for thousands of years among ruins. Later, I was standing by a side door of an unattractive palace, much like Praha's. I noticed this slob with a bestial face, then the facilitators.

"It must be the Queen's novelist," I thought. At that moment, two women in conservative suits hurried by, one of whom was Queen Elizabeth herself. They quickly disappeared into the palace. Later, I was with the group of people from the car again, this time in a health-food store. The owner of the store, who was peeling garlic cloves, mentioned that the biographical movie I wanted to see started later than I thought. "In that case," Louisa said, "I wouldn't mind sailing to Nova Scotia with these people tonight." "That's fine with me," I said, "because I still have to find the Jewish section. But you have to come back tomorrow." I stepped outside and started walking uphill. The road curved into a 1950s district, where the buildings were covered with green stone facing, not gray as in Warszawa. I wondered if this was the Jewish section.

the morning of Thursday, November 5, 1992, in Wien

At the library, I saw a suburban kid wearing a Camp Kennebec T-shirt. "You go to Kennebec junior?" I asked him. "Maybe," he said, as if he might go to senior, but I could tell he went to junior. I told him I had been the Micmac chief in their big year, 1969. Surely, he had looked at the prominent scoreboard in the dining room and noticed the Micmacs won nine, the Passys five, and everyone else had been shut out? No tribe had ever won so many, nor had so many been shut out. As I said this, I had a vision of the board as dusty, unkempt. Maybe it didn't matter anymore.

Andrew Delbanco, a graduate student in American literature at Harvard when I was an undergrad, tapped me on the shoulder on a city street. Uncharacteristically long-haired, Andy said, "I haven't seen you in a long time, not since I went to Europe and then Berkeley." I didn't think his illustrious career had taken him to those places. "Actually," I replied, "it's been longer than that. I remember the last time I saw you. It was on Mass. Ave. in front of Holyoke Center in June of '82. You made me feel guilty for not sending you my thesis on the relations between the New English and English Puritans during the English Civil War. That's why I haven't seen you in so long." Later, a young woman in the street motioned for me to follow her. She led me to a Jewish shop.

*

I was sitting in a comfortable living room with a group of teenagers. Someone's father was making all sorts of accusations about drugs. He said the phone was being tapped by the FBI. I, older and uninvolved, picked up the phone. It sounded perfectly normal, but I said, "It's definitely tapped." "Who said that? Who said that?" someone shouted at the other end of the line. I quickly hung up. Later, I was retained as a lawyer by the teenagers, even though I wasn't a criminal lawyer, only someone with a law degree. As I stood in the doorway, it occurred to me the trial might attract national attention, and I would be at the center of it. The trial was scheduled to begin the next morning, and it was already late in the evening. What should I do? Stay there with the teenagers? Go home? If I went home, I would only get seven hours' sleep, plus I didn't have any money. I wandered over to a bus stop, where, in the light from the streetlamps, I noticed a pile of coins on the ground, next to a pool of spit. The quarters were hardly wet. I swept them up and started walking through an area on the West Side, south of Lincoln Center.

the morning of Friday, November 6, 1992, in Wien

There was a problem with the new subway service supposedly between New Jersey and the Bronx. After waiting a long time for a train in New Jersey, Louisa and I had to switch to buses on 168th St. in Manhattan. After a few blocks, the bus stopped for a while. We got out and went into a store, looking for water. While we were inside, the bus drove away. We ran after it, but couldn't catch it. Another bus flew by. What should we do? After walking under a black iron railroad bridge, we entered a very leafy neighborhood. A poor boy came up to Louisa. Almost gray-skinned, in rags, he didn't seem menacing to me, but Louisa took fright. I tried to console her, at the same time worrying she would make other people come after us. "No thanks," I said hurriedly to the boy, as if I didn't understand that he was asking for something, not offering something, and we zipped away. We ran down a street with boarded-up houses, which really worried me, but no one was around. We soon entered a steamy, tropical neighborhood. Eventually, we came to a glass elevator at a steep rise in the urban terrain, slightly reminiscent of one of the A train exits in Washington Heights. Four cool types were on the elevator. They said to us, "Washington

Heights is the only place to live." Thinking the area didn't look like Washington Heights, I said dismissively, "I think I've been around here a few times before. This is near Columbia."

the morning of Saturday, November 7, 1992, in Wien

Back from a trip to Vermont, I went over to my high-school friend Steve Riegel's house. I asked Riegs how old his father was. "He's 68." "He grows flowers, right?" "Yeah." "I spend half my time thinking about flowers, too," I said. "You know, everything you say about yourself surprises me," he said. I liked the idea of that, but it worried me, too. We walked into the small living room and there was his father, right where I expected him to be. The Riegels were having a dinner party. Mrs. Riegel brought me funny, tiny shoes to put over my socks. Mr. Riegel showed a film about his Jewish ancestors. It featured battles in Eastern Europe in 1848, as Romantic as a "Three Musketeers" movie. Steve started pulling out photos at this point—one of a guy, one of a blonde, my former girlfriend Mylene Hodgson. "Remember her?" he asked. He sang a bar of "New York, New York." Then he pulled out a photo of my dead brother David's car narrowly missing another car, and two photos of me skinny, which amazed Louisa. In one, I was walking through a glass door, like my brother John did in high school at Andover. Finally, Riegs pulled out a round sepia photo of me from our high-school prom, which neither of us attended. "God, you have the best pictures of me ever taken," I said. "Do you have one of yourself like this from the prom?" "No," he said sadly. "I think I have one," I said. Leaving, we went underground into the subway. I was afraid we would come up in Bosnia, but no one was too worried about it.

the morning of Tuesday, November 10, 1992, in Wien

I was a child in a gloomy apartment who was going to be spanked. When the specified time came and went, and then more time passed, I assumed I had gotten off the hook. "When are we going out?" I asked the man there. "Hold on," he said, and he started unwrapping an object in plastic, a big wooden mallet. "You're not going to hit me with that?" I asked, afraid. "It won't be hard," he said, "we know it never really hurts in this house."

the morning of Thursday, November 12, 1992, in Firenze

A group of people were partying at my house. We were supposed to meet up with others and go to a party way out in Brooklyn, around Avenue X. Press Perlman, a friend of Mom's, decided to try to fix my turntable. I couldn't believe it when I heard it playing loud and clear after all these years. But after a few minutes, it broke again. We never met the others, either, which I felt guilty about, but my friends Deena Shoshkes and Jon Fried said we weren't to blame, the people hadn't called. Later, I found a note from Press with the stereo to the effect that the presence of smokers had ruined it; if I quit smoking and replaced certain parts, it would work again. Later, I was walking down a street with Chuck Hunter from the *Journal*, who said he never smoked anymore. He'd only had one this year. Then he said he'd just been to Budapest, actually a lovely small town outside Budapest, where some friends of friends had villas. I started to say I'd been to Budapest, but couldn't get in a word edgewise. The next thing I knew, I was at the villa, which was being fixed up. In one room, they were building a memorial to the Jews who'd been sent to Auschwitz from the villa.

the morning of Wednesday, May 12, 1993

There was an important baseball game at Kennebec senior. I was watching the hurlers, thinking they were going to be pretty tough to hit. I wondered why I wasn't I pitching. I wandered out toward right field. My high-school tennis coach, Vic Lomakin, yelled for me to come to the mound. Where would I find a left-handed glove, a team shirt? But Vic didn't want me to pitch, he wanted me and some others to put out a fire. We went to a trash pit in the woods, found some old Chlorox bottles half full of water. Walking back, I started complaining, "I was the pitcher five years ago, four years ago, three years ago. Shouldn't I still be the pitcher?" "They want to give younger kids a chance now," one of the others said. That made sense to me. Maybe it was a mistake to have come back to camp. I wondered if I quit now, a few days into the summer, what would I do with the rest of my vacation? Could we get most of our money back? I went into an old house. "Mike, Mike!" Dad called from another room. I went in. He was in a chair. "You have to help me up, my leg hardly works at all anymore," he said despondently.

the morning of Thursday, May 13, 1993

I still had more than a month to go in Rome. A young guy and I were walking around parking lots like the ones I used to blizzard with fliers for Dad's hifi store in East Brunswick. The young guy was leaving Rome. I thought about breaking down and smoking a cigarette. I thought about staying at a place where I could do a menial job in lieu of paying rent. But how would I see Rome that way? Didn't I have enough money to pay for a place, anyway? The cops came. They said, "Who threw down the banana peel?" I had, but no one said so. The cops held up a check, with a reward written out on it. An old guy ratted on me. He hadn't even been there. How did he know? The cops turned away. The old guy said I shouldn't have littered. He said I shouldn't have spit, too. I shoved him against a radiator. In the end, sitting at a big dining table, we all made up. Out on the street, there was chaos. Newsboys were flinging papers in the air.

the morning of Wednesday, August 10, 1994

At Dad's apartment after his death, I was trying to decide which paintings to take. The phone rang. It was this annoying guy Hal. I tried to fix the broken lock on the door, only making it worse. Then an alien appeared in the apartment. It was peanut-shaped—purple velvet on top and tan velvet below. When I realized it was a demon, I ran like crazy. Outside, naked, I wondered if I should go back to get some things. Like my black backpack with my poetry notebooks. "No, this is the time when you forsake everything," I told myself. The alien appeared outside and chased me.

the morning of Tuesday, July 12, 1995

I had cancer and I was going to die. I went to several doctors before I got a good prescription. I wanted to do something interesting before I died. Perhaps I should go to Europe? I talked with my boss, *Journal* copy chief Gary Ricciardi, telling him there was so much I wanted to do. It turned out Louisa had cancer, too. I needed to find the place where I got the prescription. On the way, I bumped into my first cousin, the mathematical physicist Lincoln Chayes.

the morning of Monday, August 15, 1995

Wanted by the king of my country, I hid in a mausoleum. It turned out to belong to the king's family. I ran into a blond guy, Jamie, whom I had met in Vermont in 1974, and my friend Emily Singer, who advised me to flee the country. At a car repair shop, someone was going to give me a ride to the train station in an old yellow car, but we had trouble setting up the back seat.

the morning of Wednesday, August 24, 1995

Every day before work, I was in the habit of taking a swim in the lake across the road from our office. Then we moved to a one-room schoolhouse farther away from the lake. I was worried it would make me late for work. I hitched a ride to the lake, but the driver kept going and going. The car struck a black girl sitting on a bench and didn't stop. It finally deposited me at a large outdoor plaza. I had no idea where to go. It was reminiscent of arriving at the Bois de Boulogne last year. I looked for one of those posted maps that say: You Are Here. Was this the Great South Lake? I was standing near garages that had been converted to small houses by gentrifiers. I needed to contact someone at work, so the deputy copy chief, Richard Breeden, wouldn't think I had drowned. I didn't know the new office number, a real mistake. Maybe I could call the wife of my former boss, Chris Winans? A little later, I saw my wife—it wasn't Louisa—and a blond boy. With the money they inherited after I disappeared and was declared dead, they bought one of the garage houses. My son said he never had so many toys.

the morning of Friday, September 9, 1995

A bad guy entered a crowded roadside restaurant in a rural area and made a loud announcement. I prayed he wouldn't notice me. The moment he did, he shot me. There was a huge hole in the middle of my hand! After he left, we looked at the tire tracks left by his truck in the muddy parking lot. Later, I was walking with some friends on a busy L.A. street in front of a big high school. It was the end of the school year. Lots of kids were outside. A police cruiser passed. I hoped to slip into the school to find the guy who shot me, but the metal detector was still up and running, and I had a concealed weapon. I sat outside on the curb. This time, the police pulled up beside us.

Louisa and I were climbing a mountain in Scandinavia, looking back at the water below, where there was a line of oil tankers, and lights from a surprisingly large number of settlements. At the top, even though it was very cold, we were going to sleep naked in the backseat of our Honda. "Where's Charlotte?" Louisa asked. "She's in the mountaineering hut. She'll be fine," I said. A knock on the window. A man brought over our one-year-old daughter, who was crying. Louisa wanted Charlotte to sleep in the backseat with us, but that would cramp my legs and wreck our time. "What about the way back?" I asked. "Won't she be cold?" I hit on the idea of her sleeping inside a container. I had two containers shaped like men's heads—one Uncle Leslie's, one Uncle Maurice's. The first one had Uncle Leslie's real eyes! Later, a woman political operative asked about my sister Alice. I said she was primarily an expert in running campaigns, but now she was in charge of this mountain station.

Each person in our group was riding on a sled with wheels. I noticed in the distance, alongside some high rises, this abundant wetland, and hoped we would ride there. Immediately after that, we hit a blowsy coastal lowland, unlike any place I have ever been. Perhaps like the Georgia or Florida coast. Then the road headed downhill. A leader warned us it was too steep to stop, but I was able to slow down with my feet. At the bottom, I passed some houses identified as belonging to an Indian tribe. Beside the road, I glimpsed a bunch of dead birds tied together with rope. My go-cart shot out onto a very rickety bridge made of saplings. Two Indians standing there warned me, but I couldn't understand them at first. I realized they were speaking French, saying there were dangerous fish beneath the bridge, which was liable to collapse. I tried to prevent the rest of my party, catching up behind me now, from coming onto the bridge.

the morning of Friday, September 23, 1995

France was falling to the Germans. We had to get away. On a bright day, we drove around the countryside looking for hiding places. Then we drove to a resort area, a body of land like Ortygia in Siracusa, where boat after boat was being launched with fleeing people. Louisa wanted to pile in, but I thought there was some terrible flaw in every boat. Finally, with time and boats running out, we jumped into a tiny boat—madness, really—which began deflating immediately. Maybe someone would pick us up like at Dunkirk.

the morning of Sunday, September 25, 1995

I was asked to eulogize one of my childhood rabbis, Barry Green, which created quite a quandary for me, because I couldn't think of anything nice to say about him. On the morning of the funeral, I was walking among some pavilions that reminded me of the Sackler Gallery in Washington. I paused at a small neoclassical sculptural tableau, which turned out to be the grave of the semanticist and crotchety senator, S.I. Hayakawa. It struck me as odd but not inappropriate.

the morning of Wednesday, November 2, 1995

The *Journal*'s Scott Billings and I were standing at a crossroads. He invited me to dinner with his family. Fairly soon, most of the people ran off to see a sinkhole that had developed beyond the ridge. I wanted to see Colin Powell speak. It was such a long walk to the venue with my heavy bags! I had counted on getting a ride. At the outdoor arena, I had to straddle a pole projecting from the upper deck. There were surprisingly few people. Later, on a bus, I walked to the back. I saw a guy and offered him a Miles Davis tape. He looked at it abstractedly, didn't want it. Afterward, I noticed him delving into a text that celebrated excrement.

the morning of Tuesday, November 8, 1995

I was walking eastward in far uptown Manhattan, passing through construction everywhere. "I hope they finish it all before the Republican balanced-budget amendment," I thought. Inside a gloomy building, I went up to the apartment of the poet Bruce Andrews, whom I've never met. I sat in silence a while, then posed some question. "Did I send you my questionnaire about writers?" he asked. "Joan Retallack's the only one I liked," I said. He pointed toward his bookcase, mostly French books. I stepped out with him and his friends, passed a McDonald's. I was surprised to learn he likes eating there. I split off from the experimental poets, walked past some kids hanging out. One of them had a gun. I sprinted into the lobby of a ritzy apartment building and hopped an elevator.

the morning of Monday, December 12, 1995

Uncharacteristically talking on a cellphone to my friend Mark Woldin, I suddenly saw gigantic machines headed my way. I hid beneath some pine trees. The machines went over the trees without hurting me.

＊

I climbed steep steps to a road. A woman helped me at the top. We reached the train station just minutes before our train was to arrive. She went ahead to the platform. I bought tickets, looked for cigarettes. Then I ran for the train, taking one stairway down and another stairway up to cross under the tracks. I missed the train.

the morning of Wednesday, December 28, 1995

Louisa and I were in Newark, making out. She had to leave. She was going to walk to the train station. Across the street, there was a huge ruin with guys milling around. I gave her $5 for a cab, then accompanied her to Penn Station Newark, which was deserted. I told her that in a sense, the station contained my whole life, which she didn't particularly appreciate. After the train ride, we parted in front of the World Trade Center, near my office. I kissed her goodbye on the street. "What's the matter?" I asked. "It wasn't special," she said. "Look around," I said, waving at the buildings, "we live in a mediocre world, everything about us is caught up in it."

the morning of Tuesday, January 2, 1996

I was walking in front of a dangerous high school. A kid with scraggly hair and a wispy moustache ran after me. Walked. Ran again. Eventually, I confronted him. Had I noticed the similarity of our faces? he asked. He said he was a younger version of me. Where was he in his family? I asked. It sounded like he had a bunch of brothers and sisters, as well as three children of his own. Three little girls showed up and surrounded him.

the morning of Saturday, January 6, 1996

Driving with a guy on the California coast, we passed a house that was moving on wheels, part of the set for "Hawaii Five-0." Then ruins. From an earthquake? We pulled up to a tiny beach, where we wedged into a small space. The guy had various inflatable pads. He paired up with a guy near us, and I was supposed to pair up with that guy's lover. I rebuffed the lover's advances, though I wasn't unfriendly, then I read a poetry book. The clouds overhead and the sails on the ocean suddenly mirrored each other, as in an LSD trip. My original driver went off rollerblading. I watched the sunset.

the morning of Wednesday, January 10, 1996

As we waited for a cab, I saw the great literary scholar Albert Spaulding Cook. He looked much older, thinner, with a beety face. He was walking stiffly. I thanked him for sending me his poetry book, <u>Adapt the Living</u>, all those years ago. As we drove off, Al gave us a jaunty wave through the back window.

I was leading an excursion to a poetry reading. While I was looking in an art-gallery window, one of the group came up and said she didn't want a repeat of last night. In truth, I didn't want to go to poetry tonight, I wanted to watch a video of Bob Hayes track and football highlights with Mark. Angry, I handed her the Poetry Calendar and told her to figure out what to see. I knew what I wanted. I walked past my father-in-law and others sitting on a bench, then encountered Louisa inside St. Mark's. "What's this all about?" I asked. "Last night, you made everyone look at, like, half your poetry," she said. "It was nowhere near that much!" I felt like attacking her, but walked away into another room, a gleaming café, where they had photos all over the wall of a gala for the poet Michael Palmer and the St. Mark's baseball team.

the morning of Monday, August 26, 1996

I was being chased down the broad concrete median of a highway by a guy who was going to kill me.

the morning of Sunday, April 13, 1997

At Mountain Ridge Country Club, Mark and I left Charlotte under partial supervision and wandered over to the pool, which was much larger than it used to be. Mark jumped in and swam away. I looked for the snackbar. It was outdoors now, but the management had changed and people from the Club couldn't automatically eat there anymore. A woman came up and started complaining about the snackbar. She said there was a petition going around. I said I didn't use the Club very often, but when I did, I liked to eat at the snackbar sometimes, though it didn't really matter to me. As we were talking, I pulled my bathing suit out of my bag. It was incredibly mildewed and grotty. She said she was the last of the Bicks at the Club. I mentioned Joan Bick, my Sunday School teacher at B'nai Jeshurun, but she didn't seem to recognize the name. I said one of the founders of the Club was David Sacks, "the father of my father's first wife."

the morning of Monday, April 14, 1997

I was walking down a street and suddenly had to go to the bathroom. I rang a gilt-edged glass door. A little girl appeared, followed by her mother. I didn't think the woman would open the door, but she did. Most of the first floor was a courtyard with a tropical garden. Upstairs, inside, a party was in swing, made up of arms dealers and international businessmen. After a short time, I felt a need to sneak away. On the street, I met my companion in crime, a Mexican teenager.

the morning of Wednesday, April 16, 1997

At the library looking for a map of an ancient city, I noticed a number of *Journal* people. There was something weird about the light, as if it were shining in the eyes of whoever was looking at me. Bob Dorton was there. I wondered if he was going to ask me about my newborn twins, Emily and Natalie, but he didn't seem to see me in the light. Then I saw the poet Bernadette Mayer, whom I visited two weeks ago, and walked outside with her on a lawn that reminded me of the Munch museum in Oslo. She answered each of my questions in a most noncommital way.

the morning of Thursday, April 17, 1997

My family was staying at a mansion with Louisa's aunt, Emily Wood. Downstairs, there was a big group around the dining room table. A guy showed up and loaded a pipe with something. "What is it?" someone asked. "Opium." While I was taking a hit of the opium, which I'm not sure I've ever done, he said, "Don't smoke so near the window, you'll get us busted." I looked out the window. There was a lot of activity on the street. A minute later, the room was full of plainclothes police. They herded us outside to a van. I hoped they wouldn't find Louisa upstairs. How would our newborn twins feed when they woke up? The van let us off underground near Grand Central Station. Louisa and I fell behind the others. Which tunnel should we take to catch up with the police? "Wait a minute," I said, "let's go another way and get out of here. It's not our fault." We went up to the street and hailed a cab back to the mansion. Aunt Emily was still there with the twins. I couldn't tell if the police had searched our things on the top floor or not.

✳

I went to a big outdoor party for the Bruce family, Louisa's cousins, in the country about an hour east of the city. I was standing in a grove. Three old biddies arrived. I offered to help one take off her coat. She was standoffish. I mentioned I was the late Bill Wood's son-in-law, sure that she would know him, but she didn't. Then I had to ski to the site of the party. I skied on a trail bordered on one side by a huge drop—perhaps a quarry. I reached a river that had thinner ice than the other rivers I had crossed. I fell through the ice immediately. Surprisingly, my feet didn't get wet. But a shoe fell off. I fished it out and put it on the ground beside me. A guy came along and tried to take the shoe away. "What do you think you're doing?" "You were skiing so badly," he said, "going from side to side and all." "I know I'm not much of a skier, but I haven't been in anyone's way," I said. "What jerks there are around here," I thought, and soon left the party.

the morning of Saturday, April 19, 1997

My friend Peter Baker and I were walking among the crowds in the shopping mall under Penn Station. He spotted Rod Gander, Mac's father. "We've gotta go say hello," Peter said and pulled my reluctant arm. I lingered behind, missing his first words to Rod. "You remember Michael, right?" Peter said. Rod looked at me and said, "I don't think you know who I am." "I know who you are. You're the father of Lizzie, Mac and … Jimmy. I just haven't seen you in, what, 16 years? You look totally different." He had a strong weathered look, sandy hair. He must have really changed in the past few years. Then I was looking around their house in Vermont. I felt like I was looking at the world through a dirty glass. Everything seemed dingy and sparse, like the vaunted "simpler past." Mac's mother was there, dressed very stylishly. I turned away from her and tried to remember how she used to look, imagining in fact Cynthia's mother, then turned back and couldn't fit the two people together. They told a story about a forest fire that broke out when they were away. It would have been the easiest thing to snuff out. But they returned so late that they only barely prevented the fire from reaching the house by stamping holes in the surrounding ground with a metal device. "The heat it channeled under the house helped us cook dinner," Rod joked.

I was walking downhill at night, away from a hilltop construction site where people were partying. I was vaguely trying to get away. The road snaked down through bulldozed land. Near the bottom, I realized the road stopped at a cul de sac without quite reaching the Interstate, which was in plain view. I had been down this road before and it hadn't worked out. I started back up. This sucked.

*

I was walking along a passageway with potted plants on each side—a little like the greenhouses at Longwood Gardens near Wilmington, but everything was sparser, whiter. We were given large seeds. I planted mine in an octagonal indoor garden at the foot of the stairs in my dead father-in-law's house. Then I was summoned next door to discuss politics at Steve Riegel's house. Guys were partying in honor of his coming wedding. I talked to a Palestinian who used a proverb: "This peace creates a new fighter every thirty seconds."

the morning of Saturday, May 3, 1997

Someone I wanted to avoid appeared at the other end of a long hallway in an apartment building. I shot into an elevator and pressed a button at random—I think 3. On that floor, a woman led me through several apartments. The last one had huge dimly lit rooms. I barely made out a couple of beautiful pieces of furniture—one the size of Dally's mahogany armoire. "There are so many incredibly wealthy people in Manhattan," I thought. In the last room, which was dark, two large-screen TVs were on. I noticed a woman lying in bed. She and my guide talked depressingly. There was something odd about the woman's face: She had no nose! The guide and I descended to the crowded concourse beneath the building. I spotted the two-year-old Charlotte. "Charlotte, what are you doing here?" I asked and picked her up. To surprised passersby, I said unconvincingly, "She's my sister—though we're a little different in age, like 30 years." The couple half-watching Charlotte expressed relief I was taking her off their hands. As we walked away, Charlotte said, "Mommy didn't come and Daddy fucked up."

The morning of Sunday, May 4, 1997

There were all sorts of difficulties returning to Manhattan from a night partying in Brooklyn Heights. Walking toward the Manhattan Bridge, I reached into my pocket for something, and money spilled on the sidewalk. A hard guy standing with a couple of others motioned toward the money as if to say, "It's mine now, right?" I nodded and walked in the opposite direction. There were more guys in that direction. I misplaced the Eileen Fisher bag we use for Charlotte's diapers. I walked into a hospital and noticed the bag in the lost and found. I described the contents of the bag stumblingly and showed my driver's license, but there was a hitch having to do with the fact that I had attested to Liz's birth date on her license. When I finally recovered the bag, I saw Peter and another guy, both carrying cellphones. Peter was limping from a knee injury. Did he want to go back to Manhattan with me? He brushed me off. I walked toward Flatbush Ave. and tried to hail a cab, but a group of interlopers jumped in front of me. I jogged east. There were other interlopers. Meanwhile, I encountered Peter, alone now, barely able to walk. He wanted to ride with me. I promised to pick him up. Finally, I hailed a Pakistani driver. Sooner than I expected, we reached the bridge. I should've been looking for Peter. I screamed his name out the window and ordered the driver to stop, but he couldn't stop and nearly hit the divider.

the morning of Monday, May 5, 1997

Gary Lenhardt, a poet I've never met, gave a lengthy critique of my poems while I was taking a bath. I mentioned a poem about walking along the coast, supposedly by Clark Coolidge, that I considered exemplary. Gary agreed and then surprisingly recommended Mark Strand, a favorite of my sister Kathy. Gary wanted some bread to eat. I stepped outside to buy something to spread on the bread. It turned out to be a holiday. I had to go somewhere with my family. I ran after Gary to thank him and changed my clothes at the same time. I wound up naked in his lobby. Back outside, I was picked up by a limousine with all my family inside, even my brother John. We talked about Louisa's grandfather, the diplomat Ray Atherton, who was supposedly in his 90s now. Someone said Ray had been out of date for 60 years, ever since he was 30; some people are like that. Mom was upset we weren't having a particular elderly relative to the holiday party. "This is where my friend Mitzi Augenblick had a stroke," she said, in order to gain our sympathy. At the apartment where the party was being held, I saw a horrible sight: The superannuated relative was standing in a vertical box, accompanied by several nurses. They helped her step slowly out of the box.

the morning of Thursday, May 8, 1997

On a street like the one where I lived during college, Museum Street in Somerville, workmen were carrying pieces of furniture outside to be trucked away and destroyed. Recognizing some of the pieces, I buttonholed their supervisor and complained that they were throwing away nice things. He said they were just taking junk. As each piece came out, I said something about its strong points and concluded, "Is that junk?" Every single piece had some merits. In one backyard, I noticed the huge Chinese table that Louisa's brother, Billy Wood, got when the family's house on Singing Beach was broken up. At the end of the street, I saw two white wrought-iron chairs sitting in front of a house, and I was so happy to see them again I burst into tears. I liked the idea that our furniture was making every house on the street look nice.

the morning of Saturday, May 10, 1997

At a huge coffeehouse in New Lebanon, a man was sitting in front of a laptop with a tall vertical screen. He was typing a L-A-N-G-U-A-G-E poem, which appeared letter by letter on the screen. I wondered if it was Clark Coolidge. I tried to see his face. I wasn't sure. Then I saw a black station wagon with CCC written along the side. "So it is Clark Coolidge," I thought, though I don't know for a fact that his middle initial is C. Later, there was a video program about avant garde artists in the Berkshires. I had never heard of most of them. There was an interview with one about the relationship between the Berkshires artists and the L-A-N-G-U-A-G-E poets. He said they had developed separately for a number of years before recognizing their common interests.

During a visit to a nursing home, one of the staff demonstrated some of the techniques they use. The aides put large headsets on the patients and show them videos of explosions to represent the destruction of their minds, then videos of babies crying to infantilize them.

✳

I was downstairs at my childhood home. Dad had been quiet for a long time, so I went upstairs to check on him. The door to my parents' bedroom was closed. Inside, Dad was working at his desk, balancing his checkbook. The sun was a red ball out the window. I was surprised to see the sun out at 9 p.m. I thought it had set hours ago. I went downstairs to watch the sunset from the front steps. Mom and my stepfather, Eli Pearce, walked up the driveway. I tried to tell them about my strange and wonderful overseas phone conversations with a supposed friend of theirs, a Chilean aristocrat being persecuted by his government.

the morning of Wednesday, May 21, 1997

At a camp with rough-hewn wooden buildings, someone's grandfather died. We cooked him on a campfire. I ate more than anyone else. Everything was underdone, almost sickening, but I kept eating for quite a while. I was amazed to find that people, when they're cooked, turn into square pieces of charcoal. I noticed my graduate-school friend George Kane and someone else reading through my writing. I wasn't too happy about it. They liked the notes more than the finished stuff.

the morning of Friday, May 23, 1997

I was riding a bike at night through a suburban neighborhood far outside Boston, basically lost. Another rider and I had taken a bus there. It let us off much farther from our starting point than we thought it would. It left us at an isolated diner at one of those big intersections in the middle of nowhere in the suburbs, like Wyoming Ave. and South Orange Ave. We failed to reach someone on the payphone. Then we started riding through the streets. They were such obscure, meandering suburban streets—the type it's hard to believe will lead anywhere. I couldn't see how we would ever reach the big avenues that would lead us back home through the night.

the morning of Saturday, May 24, 1997

There were some British people at a wooded estate with caves and fountains. Someone wanted to play tennis on an old grass court nearby. I fished around in my backpack, which had some wet clothes in it, and was very proud of myself for putting together a tennis outfit. Later, I was in South Orange Village, in front of the train station, looking up at the clocktower on the old police station. Ezra was telling me about an article in *Playboy*. I took a bus to a place where we were supposed to play tennis. I had trouble figuring out which was the right bus stop for Ether Street. I couldn't find any tennis courts or Brits in the huge indoor facility there, which had bars and discos and gaming tables in different buildings. In the middle of everything, I encountered Steve Hirsch, a slight acquaintance from junior high. His frizzy hair had grayed. Both of us were surprised to even recognize the other. "We've hardly ever talked," I said. Then I saw Richard Lieb, a childhood tennis rival at the Club who works for Goldman Sachs. He tried and failed to come up with my name. I walked through each of the buildings.

the morning of Wednesday, June 18, 1997

I was in a German concentration camp. I walked to where people sat around campfires, some singing. Then the Ukrainian guards started killing people. I looked for a place to sleep. I found the Russian girl with whom I had slept recently. She said that was impossible now. I found someone else, an Indian guy, but he was sleeping standing up. I would have to sleep standing up, too, and they were probably going to come and kill me during the night. I walked outside, which was dangerous, but I knew the end had come and I should at least try to get away. The next thing I knew, I was walking down a road with a fancy couple who seemed surprisingly calm. Everything was in black and white. There were these small Gothic houses on each side of the road. "Maybe we should hide in them," I thought, but then I realized with a shudder that they were mausoleums in a German cemetery. I wanted to get out of there. The young man said he had been hiding from the Germans for months. Maybe we could hide in the cemetery after all, though there could be a problem finding food. The young man said the Luftwaffe picked up the presence of people on radar and fired at them. I said you could hide deep in a cave. There must be a lot of caves here. He said the radar still picked you up, though you could get deep in some crevices, and there were interesting things hidden down there. The road came out at a huge chateau surrounded by tall trees and hedges, with many cars parked along each side of the driveway leading up to the chateau, and around the circular drive on the right side of chateau, but no people outside in the night. I was worried Germans would appear at any time. I noticed the date on a small sign: January 1, 1945. I thought it was later than that, in May of 1945. By this time, I had turned into the fancy young man. A silvery woman, Alice Roosevelt Longworth, met us at the top of the front steps. Suddenly, I felt like I was in an old movie, something on AMC, or Rainer Werner Fassbinder's "Veronica Voss." Alice Roosevelt Longworth only talked to the fancy young woman, socialite talk. She asked what my companion had been doing in New York lately. At the end, she added to my companion's account, "And a little modeling, I bet." "I never modeled," my companion insisted. As for me, the silvery lady said, it would be hard to find a place for me here. It was full of people like me. The Germans carefully checked out who was here. But she had an idea. I was to work in PB. I thought about the initials, decided they meant Postal Business. "That's a good, necessary place to work," I thought, "I won't attract much attention." At the end of our interview, as we were walking past, the silvery lady whispered to my companion, "He's proposed, I hope. ... Good." Inside, things were back in color. My job required me to deliver papers and pick up papers in an endless warren of windowless offices, primitive places with things stored in wire baskets on the walls. They were staffed by sloppy men, some of whom were sympathetic to my plight. There was a good camaraderie overall.

the morning of Friday, August 15, 1997

On my way to work, George Kane handed me a packet of leaflets promoting Peter's contemporary poetry anthology, Onward. I wasn't planning any such campaign for my first poetry book, At an Intersection. I couldn't hand out any of the leaflets because I was moving tonight. I went to Louisa's to pick up some stuff. The people upstairs brought down some incredibly slimy things of mine. Why didn't they just keep them? I drove the stuff in a truck, but had to park a few blocks away from the new place. I emptied everything out on the city sidewalk— there were a bunch of scraggly plants, a couple on their last legs, remnants of my vast collection of house plants during high school. Louisa had to decide which ones to jettison. I had to move everything out of my house now.

the morning of Sunday, August 17, 1997

A group of us, including Gary Lovesky, were told to lie on the ground and die. It wasn't that big a deal, but we were supposed to lie a certain way. When rigor mortis set in, my limbs weren't in the correct position. I tried to straighten them, but I couldn't. I didn't want this rigor mortis.

✳

Steve Kurens and I had both moved back to South Orange. I thought it was really nice that we both had grown up in the town, and that of all the places in the world to live, we had both come back to it. But I was disturbed to find my journal from the spring of 1981 in Cambridge flaking apart in a garbage can outside my new house. That shouldn't be thrown away.

the morning of Monday, August 18, 1997

There was a series of concerts in Boston and New York between a Thursday and a Saturday, which caused all kinds of logistical problems. For example, on Thursday evening, there were no trains to Boston after 7:15, and I get off work at 7. I don't know how I reached Boston that night, but I did. There was some kind of orientation at a day-care center, where I saw Michael Palmer, whom I met once a few years ago. "You're not one of the people who believes that all personal violence stems from political violence, are you?" I asked. "I do," he said. Later, we saw the first of a series of concerts celebrating German composers. I was surprised that would appeal to Michael Palmer. The first concert was an unexciting late 19th century work. I had to hurry back to New York for the next event. By accident, I wandered into a room where immigrants were being detained. As I was about to leave, I noticed in my car trunk a box of somewhat-crushed sticky buns, a breakfast treat among Louisa's family in Philadelphia.

the morning of Wednesday, August 20, 1997

I visited the elderly Babe Ruth in his apartment downtown on the east side of Manhattan. He was in very good shape, very easy to talk to. Subsequently, I encouraged a black woman who was writing a biography of Ruth to go interview him. Then I went back to see him again, but his building had turned into a rundown housing project. I finally found his name on the directory of one of the buildings, but it turned out that he and his wife were in a hospital ward inside. Their condition was rated "poorest." Over her rating, it said "regrettably." I had to fill a prescription for him, which was a problem, because I was going to Washington for the weekend. But the doctor assured me that his condition wasn't so bad.

the morning of Monday, September 8, 1997

I spent some time with an older German woman, who had once been a refugee from her country for many years. Now it was my turn to be a refugee, fleeing the Nazis. She told me the name of her village in the far north near Rostock and hoped I would be able to find her after the war. In my flight, I had to cross several quadrangles where I was afraid I would encounter soldiers. How could I explain what I was doing, someone clearly of draft age? Inside, at a newsstand, I decided to buy some rolling tobacco for my flight. A package of Drum cost one franc. I wasn't sure if I had any francs. How many marks? 14. Germany's currency was sure going down the tubes as it started to lose the war. I reached into my blue daypack and came up with five French francs and three Belgian francs. I decided to buy three packages of tobacco, but the people behind me in line were snapping them up, too. One guy tried just to buy the rolling papers from a package of Bugler. I succeeded in getting three packages of Drum, but then the lights dimmed and I couldn't find my daypack, where I had put the tobacco.

the morning of Tuesday, September 9, 1997

Our group, led by former Turkish premier Tansu Ciller, was under constant assault from opponents, getting smaller and smaller. Even our kids at school were being indoctrinated against us, learning math in the morning and English in the afternoon. Liz, still a kid in South Orange, told me all about it.

the morning of Wednesday, September 10, 1997

I had two small houses with a courtyard between them, like my grandparent's place near Tanglewood. I built a little structure in the courtyard. A friend came and added to the structure. The two parts went together so well. We had a talk in which he noted that my senior tutor at Harvard, Prudence Steiner, "made sure you read a lot" for the honors written examination. After he left, I sat down and wrote a story about him and me building this structure and then becoming lovers. It disturbed me very much.

the morning of Thursday, September 18, 1997

My family was staying in a small house with low ceilings on a flat road like Route 20 in New Lebanon. There was something unnecessarily cramped about the space. At the front door, we saw off this disturbing woman who had been visiting us. When I turned around, I saw under the couch a pair of white high-heeled shoes, perhaps the shoes the woman had been wearing. Then the creepiest thing happened. I looked closely at the shoes and saw ankles. Ample legs. There was a woman hiding under the couch. I reached in, but she disappeared. Where was she now? I knew she was somewhere.

the morning of Sunday, September 28, 1997

My high-school graduation was being held inside Columbia High School, not at the football field, where it was held in fact. For some reason, my mentally ill brother, Stephen, was also graduating. Mom had given me a key to give Steve. Without the key, he couldn't graduate. I was standing outside school talking to some people. I noticed Steve nearby. He was wearing a white dress shirt without a tie, the way he used to dress in high school. We talked. He seemed to be doing very well. Inside, a performance was already going on. I eased into an empty seat between some people in the balcony. It was a modern dance performance with the poet April Bernard's husband, Marc Robinson, in the star role as a Chinese dragon writhing around the stage, making histrionic facial expressions. I didn't know he was a performer. I thought he was only a scholar. He's also a choreographer, someone said, though his reviews are mixed.

the morning of Tuesday, October 7, 1997

I was planning to visit my stepfather's polymer-chemistry colleague in Hungary, Mr. Pongor, which Louisa and I failed to do in 1992. Intellectually, I was on the trail of 1968. What should I read? Norman Mailer's Armies of the Night? This would be a good time to read that. I went up to the third floor of our house to find the book. Owen and Knox Cummin were sitting on the white couch. I "accidentally" lurched and dropped a heavy object on them. Later, I ran up the stairs and "accidentally" slammed into Owen. "We have to stop this," he said, and he was right, violence wasn't going to do any good.

the morning of Wednesday, January 14, 1998

On the day after New Year's, I went fishing in my long-dead brother David's waders. A strong current prevented me from returning home. I struggled against it to no avail, then decided to go with it. The river washed me way downstream, but always near the bank, not out in the middle. On land, I walked several miles home through unfamiliar villages, stopping at a gas-station convenience store for something to eat.

the morning of Sunday, February 8, 1998

My brain flickered out, once, twice, and each time I brought myself back. What did it feel like? It felt like the time in the summer of 1979 when a guy had a stolen tank of nitrous oxide at Mt. Auburn Cemetery in Cambridge, and I inhaled a balloon of it and blacked out.

the morning of Monday, March 2, 1998

I was taking a bus home, but not in Brooklyn. The place had the feeling of a Long Island suburb. Also an Italian feel. The bus reached the intersection of many roads. I should have gotten off there. Then it angled to the right through the huge intersection. I thought it was going to stop at an island partway across. That would be fine, because the island basically flowed into the street I was going to walk on. But the bus didn't stop there, it continued all the way across the intersection and then pulled into the parking lot of a mall. I was far away from where I wanted to go. I got off. The bus driver yelled at me for getting off too soon. We had a brief exchange and I said in Italian, "It's better to do what you say you're going to do." He liked that, he liked that a lot. Others started getting off. Suddenly, a group of policeman with drawn guns ran into the big department store. There was a shootout with robbers. I hit the deck. In a lull, I tried to dash out of the parking lot and regain my course home. The shooting started up again. I crouched between cars. The robbers headed in my direction. "If they see me," I thought, "they'll shoot me."

the morning of Friday, March 6, 1998

I murdered two women, maybe more. I strangled one woman after she ran screaming out of a storefront. Earlier in the day, I had killed another woman in a less noticeable encounter. I also stalked and fired shots at several woman downstairs in my house, but somehow that didn't count on my roster of crimes. After the murders, I went into an empty warehouse where some black gangsters were being arrested. It didn't seem to bother them much. Apparently, I knew them. I helped myself to a bowl of chocolate soft ice cream from an open vat. As I was leaving, some people started shouting that I should be in jail, too. Walking home, I had the most peculiar feeling: "Right now, I'm free, but I'm going to be imprisoned for the rest of my life, I'll never get out." The thought pained me so much. I knew the earlier killing might not be pinned on me, but there was so much evidence against me in the strangling. It was amazing I hadn't been charged yet. I wondered if it ever happens that there's a killing and no one looks into it very closely. No, not here.

the morning of Tuesday, March 10, 1998

Some kids threw snowballs at me as I walked past South Orange Junior High and the duck pond, carrying one of my twin babies. It wasn't a big deal. But then the kids followed me up a path into the woods. Mark joined me. We scared the kids off badly. Mark wanted to engage them some more. But I said tendentiously, "We should stay away from them before they do harm, because they have the capacity to do harm."

*

There was loud knocking at the door. I peered out the window and saw a tall, unkempt man. He tried to break down the door. I ran to call 911 while Louisa cowered with the kids in the hall. I wanted to speak loudly into the phone, so the bad guy would be scared off, but my voice utterly failed me, the way my body used to go rubbery in dreams when someone ordered me to do something.

the morning of Saturday, March 14, 1998

I was walking up a scary road late at night, raked by headlights. Then I descended to a park, a little larger than Grove Park in South Orange, the first park of my childhood. I quickly calculated the safest way to walk through it. But I was surprised to find a lot of people there, peacefully playing, at that time of night. I instantly relaxed. It was like some utopia. But as I was walking through, a man attacked me. He was grubby and stocky—with sexual designs, I think. I dodged him and tried to get the people to help me, but they pretended not to notice.

the morning of Friday, March 20, 1998

We were watching a movie being made on a train platform, which had an elevated track overhead. When the movie was over, Ezra had to catch a train. Later, he sent a fax saying everything had turned out OK. Louisa threw it in the garbage, where grease got on it. I fished it out and criticized her in front of Ez's wife, Jane Hammerslough. Then I went to work, where I uncharacteristically shirked something or other. In the newsroom, a woman walked up to me and asked if I remembered her. She was so familiar. Her older face seemed to wash away, her young face come shining through. Except that her nose had been flattened. That was different. Her name was on the tip of my tongue. She looked away. When she looked at me again, I said, "Karen Hirschberger." There was some sexual innuendo between us, not surprisingly. Then I was walking down steep metal steps outside. Below, a train was pulling into the station. Louisa, on the platform, waved for me to hurry down. I tried to push myself, but it was hard with a backpack, and my legs weren't working properly! At the bottom of the stairs, the back of the train was still a good distance away from me. I was never going to make it. The train started moving just before I reached it. Louisa and I both waved at the train. It stopped. It actually backed up. Rapidly. Now, I had to run back to the passenger cars—there were so many engine and mail cars before them. Oh no, the train started moving forward again. But then it stopped when the first passenger car reached us. We had made the train.

the morning of Thursday, April 30, 1998

Reading a poem by Louis Zukofsky, I saw the words literally come to life. As my eyes passed over them, the words moved like ants or flaming embers. Then the words died down, to an ashy white, and the next clump of words came to life. My eyes were like a fire or an animating fluid.

I walked up a path from the ocean to some people's house, where we had left our three-year-old daughter, Charlotte. Then I took a walk across a field. Men on horseback were riding through. They tangled with a bull. The bull caught sight of me. It was definitely going to attack. I called out to the horsemen. They wouldn't help. My legs went rubbery, but I was able to hide behind a bony, leafless bush. Afterward, I walked around the land, looking at the amazing number of houses being put in. The land was filling up with houses overnight. Then, Louisa and I drove on a long straight road—I'm tempted to say a Belgian road—to her dead father's house, though the place was nothing like his farm. Inside a dusty cobwebbed hall with lots of furniture, I said, "Let's see what this stuff is." "It's all junk," Louisa said. I tried my cigarette lighter. She flicked on a switch. More lit up than should have. Everything looked nice at first glance, but deteriorated instantly under scrutiny. Even the bookcases. There was a basket of old dolls, dolls from before my time. "Take some," I said. "OK," Louisa said, taking one. There were model ships, but made from some cheap material, a precursor of modern plastics. Then we went into her parents' room. Horror: There were two monstrous twin babies on a bed, hydrocephalic, totally unlike EmmyNatty. Nearby, there was another huge baby. "Let's get out of here," I said. "They're our babies," she said. "No, they're not." Louisa walked toward them. "Don't!" I yelled. Then they turned into kids from a wholesome old movie. "When are those clothes from?" Louisa asked. "Sometime earlier in the 20th century." Suddenly, the babies vanished, leaving us with the cobwebbed room and the bed. Then we visited one of her relatives' estates, which had been turned into a museum. I picked up some old-fashioned consumer item, a cracker tin or the like. A guard asked me if it was mine. Louisa went off walking around the grounds with her sister, Maude. What about Charlotte? Where was Charlotte? We hadn't accounted for her after the play date. She was on her own somewhere. I found out she had entered a gay bar.

the morning of Tuesday, June 2, 1998

My dead brother's girlfriend, Susan Ei, lived in an old farmhouse that was in increasing disrepair. The wall had fallen off a whole section. It was very cold in winter. Susan showed me some organic vegetables she was cooking. I admired her energy, but she said she wanted to do less, especially now that it was colder. Her mother was going to prepare a newborn calf that had arrived in a gauzy covering. There would be enough food for anyone who showed up. Before the meal, bells rang. Did we want to go to the huge church in the center of the community? It seemed to be something of a cult. Tom Walker and I sat together, skeptical. Outside, an acolyte monk took us on a tour of the compound. He showed us a film clip of Henry Ford promising to contribute to the church's efforts. Then he showed us a new piston—apparently purchased with the gift. He led us around a deserted convent that used to belong to a group similar to theirs. At one point, the convent had been sold and all the sisters' graves had been exhumed and moved to their graveyard. But now, they had enough money to buy the convent and were moving the graves back. Why bother? I wondered. Standing at the bronze front doors of the convent, with a big view in several directions, Tom and I decided to leave.

the morning of Tuesday, June 16, 1998

A novel of mine had been published many years ago by Picador, publisher of the translation I have of Elias Canetti's Auto da Fe. I had no recollection of writing it. The novel was from the immediate period after Cynthia and I broke up in early 1983, but it was very oblique, hard to see how it referred to my life then. The pages looked like the pages of Louis Ferdinand Celine's Death on Credit, especially some telltale ellipses in the second section. The book also had some connection with Fyodor Dostoevsky's Notes From the Underground and Witold Gombrowicz's Cosmos (not the style of novel I could ever write). It was quite a mystery to me. Maybe I had the dimmest memory of writing it. How could I remember so little? I looked for it at a big library with Mom, the Newark Public Library of my childhood. After I found it, I walked through a long hall in the library wondering if anyone still read the novel. What happens to novels published 15 years ago? Later, I was at a table in a restaurant near a big group of people, including Louisa's late uncle, Clement Biddle Wood Jr., a satiric novelist. Later still, I was wandering around the outside of a small house with Mom. I wondered if Cynthia had any awareness of the book.

the morning of Wednesday, July 1, 1998

I rode a motorboat on glassy waters from a southern island all the way down to Antarctica. When it was time to return, I had a hard time reading the map and figuring out which route to take back. It was getting later in the day. The ocean seemed to be getting rougher. My college friend Harris Collingwood was there. Maybe the best thing was not to try to go back now.

the morning of Friday, August 28, 1998

I was waiting for Mom outside an apartment building in an urban area. A guy pulled a knife on me. He talked a mile a minute about what I needed to do to avoid being stabbed. I couldn't understand whether he wanted me to stay or go. His knife wasn't far from my abdomen. "This might be the end of my life," I thought. Finally, he said something that suggested I should run away. But when I ran up the street, he shook his head, as if to say I had made a mistake. Mom came outside then. Not worried about her, I started running up the street again, but my thighs were as heavy as rocks. It didn't matter. The guy didn't run after me.

The morning of Saturday, October 24, 1998

Louisa and I were looking at a big new apartment. The bedroom was a disaster. It was going to need all sorts of work on the upper walls and ceiling, probably new molding. I decided we wouldn't have Mike Streaman do it. Then I was talking to Streaman, who, it turned out, owned the apartment. "This won't be a handshake deal," he said. "It sure won't," I said, "I need to have the rules of the co-op." "I'll just take care of that stuff," he said. "No, you won't." In the apartment, some workmen had torn down a wall of the bedroom, creating a large room, and were putting green shag carpet on the upper part of the wall! Wasn't the place bigger than this? Bigger than one large room and a kitchen someplace? Looking for the kitchen, I wandered into a whole series of beautiful rooms, with plants and a piano and loveseats and a fancy bathroom. I came out in the original large room and crossed it to a very odd area where there seemed to be the remains of an industrial kitchen and this bizarre copper water slide down to the glassed-in first floor. If we took out the slide, we'd have a long narrow space two stories' tall to work with. What would we do with it? Later, on the ground floor, I was in a car, talking with Louisa's friend Janet Murray through an open window. A cop came. I started to leave. Janet's finger got caught in the window as I closed it. I noticed the glassed-in first floor bordered the street, wondered about the security. I saw an alarm-system strip, but was worried nonetheless. The place was on the Upper West Side, around 74th St. A street sign nearby said Mud St. Louisa appeared in a car. She'd been forced to drive the wrong way down an endless tunnel. How much were the fines—$191? $291? Or $391? $391. I asked how much the apartment cost and she said $500,000. I said this was one of those multimillion-dollar New York apartments in the long run, though it needed a lot of work.

the morning of Monday, October 26, 1998

A young woman who resembled our old babysitter Allison from Bay Ridge, but had odd stitches around the outside of her face, told me enthusiastically about video gambling. She took me out in New York Harbor, where there was a gambling boat near the Statue of Liberty. She sat at a terminal and showed me how to get on. I sat at the terminal next to her and asked a bunch of stupid questions. She didn't want me sitting so close to her, for sexual reasons, and asked me to move over to the next seat, which was fine with me. Later, I asked her about the stitches, and she said, "It's being—" "—What?" "They pull off the face and smooth all the acne off, that's all I can afford." She pointed to her acne, which I didn't think looked so bad, and said, "I shouldn't have to live with skin like this."

the morning of Thursday, April 15, 1999

I was having coffee with my late cousin Mann Genchell at a sidewalk café in Williamsburg. Mann ordered a seltzer. I followed suit. The waiter brought me a dirty glass half-full. I resolved not to pay for it. For some reason, Mann had to leave. I went for a walk by myself around Harvard. In an upper part of the campus, beyond a police guard, there were Roman ruins. Why hadn't I looked at them as an undergraduate? Maybe because they were beyond the law school, on a part of the campus where we rarely went. I suddenly worried I would bump into Owen and Eleanor. But with 100,000 other people living in Cambridge, that wasn't likely. On the other side of the hill, there was a huge sloping lawn. The corner of a lake was visible at the bottom, with people swimming on this hot day. I headed downhill on my bike. On a spit of land dividing the lake from the ocean, the tide was rising over the land. In the distance, I noticed Owen and others in the cove of a private swim club. I ditched my bike and swam along the coast, with the idea of annoying them. I did annoy them, though not as much as I wanted to, and the lifeguard or swim instructor pompously told me it was a private club. Heading back, I walked on land and then was surprised to discover myself at the top of a tower supposedly owned by Mark's friend Jim, an Upper West Side drug dealer. How did I get so high above the ground without realizing it? I started down the back steps, but they were terrifyingly steep, practically a ladder. Was there another way? The stairs I'd come up. Which was safer? "The one built most recently," Jim said. I went and looked at the back steps again. A ginger ale bottle had been left on the third step down, just what I'm always telling Louisa and Mom not to do. I decided to go down the other way. Since Jim had been nice to me, I invited him to visit us in Brooklyn. Looking for a piece of paper to write down my address, I pulled out a notebook with Japanese characters on each page and some writing beneath, probably by the French poet Victor Segalen. It was very beautiful. I wrote down 433 4th St. Jim, repeating the address aloud, said 434. I crossed the number out and wrote it again, and now it really looked like 434. I crossed that out and then I wrote 433 3rd St.! I couldn't get it right.

the morning of Saturday, August 14, 1999

My family was boating in a Maine bay. Natalie was hanging over the side in the cold water. I had to make some complicated hand moves to save her. Then, we were in a house in a suburban neighborhood. Charlotte was in another house, up a hill from ours. I went to get her, and she was driving down in a car by herself! Through a picture window in our house, we saw a cloud of dust coming from the façade of the new retail building across the street. Dust came in our open door. It didn't seem so bad. But when Charlotte went to play in the doorway, I screamed for her to come back, and right after that, the new building collapsed, flinging bricks into the open door. Then, we were in a gloomy master bedroom that supposedly belonged to Louisa's father's cousin, Philip Fisher, in Maine. There were weird Victorian objects on the night table, including versions in different kitschy media of the sculpture of dancing satyrs that used to be at Bill Wood's farm. There was a photo of men lying in bed from a St. Paul's School reunion. I wondered if one man in particular was Bill. The photo actually came to life and the man shifted his head, so I could tell it was Bill. Then, I saw a picture on the mantel of a Wood family trip to Rome, Louisa's grandparents Emily and Clement Biddle Wood at the Forum, his jaw jutting out the way it usually did. Was that the young Uncle Clem and Aunt Emily in the foreground? Where was Bill? In a woman's handwriting on the back, it said: "1935 was a bad year for the family."

the morning of Thursday, August 26, 1999

I discovered a secret room off the first floor of our house. It was full of furniture that must have been left there by previous owners. I craned my neck into the long narrow room, which had some curious pieces—oddly colored glass tables—as well as some antiques, but nothing that valuable. Part of the house's woodwork was bashed in near the entrance to this secret room, just as it was upstairs, outside another similar room. Louisa seemed annoyed by the existence of the room. She pulled several pieces of furniture out into the hall "as a precautionary measure."

the morning of Thursday, November 11, 1999

I was reading an odd long poem supposedly by a friend of my aunt, Antonia Handler Chayes. There was something in it about the future world that I didn't understand, but when I asked Aunt Toni about it, she didn't remember giving the poem to me. I walked out onto the terrace of Aunt Toni and Uncle Abe's house in Cambridge. It looked onto Harvard Square, unlike their real house on secluded Hubbard Park Rd. "A lot of people must walk past here in other seasons," I thought. Then I hung around the kitchen, not sure if I was hoping for a dinner invite. At a key point, I said I was going to someone else's house, and Aunt Toni and Uncle Abe invited me to stay. At the table, my plate was too near one of their young girl nieces. Aunt Toni came over and pushed the plates apart. At that moment, Uncle Abe got a phone call from Dad about my brother Sandy. Uncle Abe looked very upset, exclaimed, "I can't believe Sandy Ruby's dead." I stood up, wandered around, saying, "Oh God, this one time, make it untrue." It was untrue.

INNER VOICES HEARD BEFORE SLEEP

W HEN I WAS A SENIOR IN COLLEGE, I took a course devoted to the writings of Sigmund Freud, taught by Professor Philip Hoffman in the sinister William James Hall on Kirkland Street in Cambridge. During that semester, I wrote down my dreams for the first time. I also noticed for the first time that as I was falling asleep, I would briefly hear sentences spoken by different voices, a few of which I recognized, such as my own or my mother's. Four years later, when I spent a week alone before Christmas on Benefit Street in Providence, writing experimental poetry for the first time, I learned how to hear the inner voices at will. Lying on the couch, with a view of the Narragansett Electric plant through the bare trees, I would clear my mind of all thoughts and listen for a very particular sound, the sound of sand being poured on sand. The inner voices would begin as soon as I heard that sound. I found that after two or three inner voices, I would invariably fall asleep. To transcribe them, I had to pull myself back from sleep continuously. Edgar Allan Poe, in "Marginalia," describes a similar process with "visions" seen "only when I am upon the very brink of sleep." These are the first inner voices I transcribed:

How hard for it to be done
Oh, I see
7 a.m. to 7 p.m.
It's the way he's doing that
…take Angela
There's no room for a boundary—do you know?
You sound optimistic to me, David

After that winter, I transcribed inner voices roughly once a year for the next 15 years. Then, in 1999, I thought it might be worthwhile to transcribe a whole book of inner voices, taking more extensive dictation. I eventually came to view the book as forming the third part of a trilogy with Fleeting Memories and Dreams of the 1990s, documenting three "varieties of unconscious experience," unlike C.G. Jung's similarly titled Memories, Dreams, Reflections in the English translation, which is a classic autobiography.

I have always tended to believe the inner voices originate outside me, perhaps as microwave broadcasts picked up by silver mercury fillings in teeth, as one of my college mentors, the 1950s novelist and conspiracy theorist H.L.

"Doc" Humes, used to teach long before the existence of cellphones and wifi. But they might be fragmentary conversations overheard and preserved in the course of life. They might be chatter created by the brain, just as the brain creates dreams. They might be some mixture of the three. They might be something else entirely. Whatever they are, I like the idea that we have this stream of voices flowing deep within us, rarely if ever heard. Each transcription could begin and end with ellipses, a minuscule segment of the continuous stream. More important from the point of view of poetry, the inner voices almost always speak a sentence or a phrase—a line. If the line is the unit of inner voices, then inner voices are a psychic underpinning of poetry, one of the ways poetry is embedded within us. We have this continuous multivocal poem "streaming" within us, only audible in the briefly inhabitable borderland between waking life and sleep.

1

Everything else is set up
If this is why I sent you
They'll come

Four, please
Go on, now it's gone

The fingers are down
The necks
And we have cereal once a week

I might all of a sudden disappear
The match

Do you want to give yourself up to me?
What the guy was giving up
What did we say about that?
Hang around for which sister?
Who else would want it?
To make sure she won't forget it

Don't worry
It very well could be
Um
Really
OK-OK-OK
He's a great guy
OK

Garrine, do you know?
Stephen Kern

Yell and give me a call
I would let you know

Mino
I mean

Did you know his name is Farino?
John Stern is not one of his many friends
Try Kenny
Sirocco

I worked the day before so much
I have far too good friends in this school
That's one of the problems waiting for you

He comes down last night
Very funny, right
No, no-no-no-no
He didn't scream
Today, he isn't screaming

This I heard this morning
You might want to keep it

Wanting space-space-space-space-space
She has New York, hunh?
It is, it is
On my floor

2

We listened to the music for too long
And Gus and I were playing

It's on it
Pittsburgh

Trouble is
The rock, the fly

And the song is
The citation
The thing is, have you ever heard?

Woodlawn Cemetery, please
Outfitters for the rich
I'm gonna give them three
Or one
Or maybe two

The natural, denying messenger type

It seems OK now that it's almost over
Should be used by crooks
The household business
Hearsay
Not me
Some of it is doubtful

He starred often on the day
I don't think that's accurate
I'm sure you know how you're gonna present this
Could you just tell me?
Why you got to teach?

3

...and he's partially asleep

The whole score on how to be successful officers
Don't get upset over coastal puzzles
We had to match so much yesterday at sea

I took some money
I guess they take their money
Four hours a day, how much?

The underwear off
White Plains

I tell ya, if I was six minutes away
Tonight, I'm gonna have some problems
They're still lookin' forward to that—

Tell Mrs. Van Eager
June
June, June, June

The Kings' argument
You know, we're just angry at you
Chillmar, Chillmar
Chillin', Chill

Despite the name, it's really the first I thought
Why?
I don't know
I don't know
Grumblers had loads of things to change
I'm just checking if you can feed them

4

Everybody's sick and I don't know what to do

Vision, vision
A different kind of airlift

Three and call
Help the Braves, baby
Closing league

Time and anger
A deal is a deal
I don't know the situation
In appearances

Yes, I are
Coming down the stretch, they do

This was a big problem

You are
You are us
What you told them
At some deep place
The bond was cracked and the Pomona iced
Together, that amounts to
Feasible

Now do come back, combatants
To my apartment
These are words deep in your soul
A wood sword episode

Every morning, as you can see
Stand up and—
After Sidney was born
Hopefully, I am loved so much that—

Where in two weeks?
Breeding
Very strong reasons

5

She's not an idiot or nothing
On product safety
He played the botanicals

Very simple, and very easy to get off
Did you notice?
The saw about the idea
Well, the idea
To quit the pair a day early
The only thing that mattered
Oops, it did

The thoroughness is possible
The boiling isn't
They angry
And Hugo
Hugo
Hugo elapses

Did you like yesterday?
Dick or better
Get 'em up
Foot 'em up

There's a bank here
Salmon goes down
There's someone who goes this way
For these things, we didn't have time
It did not go to solicit
Other than whatever I sent over

You just can't help listening
Another historian's attack
Stay alive as soon as possible
And the meaning of my work ceased

We made transitions

Brush it now
Brush it now means never to tie your teeth
Everyone who saw it knew they had to change

If you don't think, there won't be any more partridge
Pare the request
Nah

And that meant not for the other judges either
Bring in some decent jokes
Want po-leece officers sittin' next to you?

6

With this, I think, the big inclination is
This is cigarettes

Airplane dust
When you're right

Grandma's house

Mumford
Here, he says
The lead
Mountain gale
Has he passed?

Chile con carne
That kind of stuff

Westerward
But even
Reagan's whole package

Who is?
Stop Bogey's

I have found postcards possible because they have received a—

You're so much fun
Water's still in there?
You don't know damn well
To him, I better go back

A core of murder
Dancing around
Flash the water
What else to do?
Just help
The clothes off this one

Tyranny, could we?
Termini?
But anyway
So as to believe you
What duh yuh wan'?
Carney's new hostess

I'd done nothing disastrous after this
In the sand very well

What kind of juice is this?
Not the only
You can see how these things work
I seem to be organizing that

Nice to hear your voice
Um-hum
It's such a nice thing
Our time is right
Our health is second

Poor guy
The food's new
Miscues
Our million
I'll say it
Clear me, too
So, he's a better guy
Gentle

It will be against you
A lot better

Steve Young has to evaluate
If you get more, do more
Barry Sanders retired and disappeared
Isn't that stubborn?
He's 20 years older than I am

There's two Eliot Goodwins for everyone else

Daddy, what's a—
No one wants to know
Yo, assume

7

Put money on the thing

What states do you have in mind?
States on the edge of sleep?

You'll go to state prison

This ambulance is a—
Solely, for the express purpose
Why is it—
Oh, we will find it
Yeah, and I suppose you're right
Without the proper
Perhaps you were
For this weekend

You did that Spanish article
But the dogs

Be quiet and reverse some people
He could go backwards through time, way through time

8

Hotfoot came and went
Sombreros
In the organ
All of these days
Here then, make a story out of it
The way the rain came

9

You know what they said?
What?
A lot of time and energy
To throttle them
And wisdom

What's the horizon for?

Stay upstairs
Until
The final speaker

At times, it seemed forced
Against Douglas
Anyway

To be telephoned
Following the election

If they wanted to take you back there
They would
I wouldn't go

Stand on such a chance
Or something's going to have to be done about it

The painting
Or whatever
You didn't do something else

This zone is so easy
The next zone is easy, too

The wild
Later on this week

A Spanish cobra

Why sink it?

I sat down and discussed with you
Look into yuhself

I told you this story
The woman is very bearing

To set things straight
Developing

I don't want to think of myself as a Yankee
So just cancel

I've had health problems all my life
Also, that
Responses have gone up
Five years already

10

Beautiful
Beautiful
And beautiful

One can see the millions he added by taking on—
That's economic stuff
You figure

11

At the White House
You just can't
You're not supposed to

Why isn't he?
Here

The highest

And he's said nothing about the future of America
And the implications

There's no point in interviewing

JC said
You can only take one man
(These are good)

You don't really know
Are you doing it right?

There's no legend
Oh
Hired

If we do what we said
Five or six strong republics

He did a demonstration
Of nobody yet
With the money

Assistance learning
Struggling sufficiency

On the booby head

It just passes through watching television

Well
He's making canapes
The smoke

Better criticism
…reads his ass off

He makes time at the end of it
To play synagogue

The Baltimer

As eyes against him
Well, let 'em
Hades

I'm not enjoying the feeling in my body
Or swing

All kinds of teachers and throwbacks
We might have thrown you into the fire

He's a lighter—
Teachers
Then school systems

Based on this one
Goin' for his future

I don't want to nurse you out
Some of which we've already decided

I just can't focus
Can you screw its—
Goose

The histories
First theme: I'm going to have to do it

Soap
Soap kills

The basketball cable
The total in my voice

If he tied you
You tied me

Could you tell me what the name of the kangaroo poodle is?

Unless you tell me what to do
I'll write you down

They are nuts
His book's out

By me
Beautiful days
Sure

Haunted
That word
Please
The luxury

Build up one guy
Backfires other days

So he can
He can
He has another fancy brow

The outside chances are insignificant
What we're doing for doom's sake

Do you hear the speed of it?

Who say yes?
Who say now?
His 'stituency

Another vote for Sloater
Sloater

This hour
Reasons were down 2%

What's the issue?
What?

Face the wind with me
And the smallest de-tails

I don't know how you do it
It's not easy
It's not easy

12

We've been waiting
Meeting and going
President of I guess it was—
The story tells me a thousand words

Crispy
Right through

When Ozzie failed
You followed him when Ozzie fell

Cowherd
Prosper

The first time around
Stop me when you're able
It stirs you out of it
Don't you?
So you don't have hotel lights in there
And guys who like
A rough and tough and yonder

13

Oh God
You look further

Beloved employees of the job

Each has a count

North American fair
Profit

The village heritage and the valley

Freely in those talks
Did you see the last one?

A piece of—baboon
Forests
Clothes

Once we felt that—
He's never been before
Had never been

Jewish holidays in the world
Knockio
Salad

Decline in power
In position

14

Let us say
I look at you now in a different light

What did he say?

The lazy man's period
Some leftover

In your veins you're a street
Addressing rooms

Party pay
Who knew?
You pay the same price

The legitimate
Or the other thing—

It was also really smart
Not to sue me

That was Steinbone's idea
I'm gonna sue you
Steal your eyes

Until someone addresses it
We've got to start over, too

The possible loan
Possible change

Afternoon, you can't get 'em like that
They don't come like that

See, it's the other way
Yeah
The other one

Oh, you kidding?
No, I am not

Oh, you can, Daddy
Here is my gas

If you want to buy a limousine
Or see something in basketball

The water fell so low
Goddamn
I found it so low to stay in sync

Don't tell me why they'd like to do the surgery or not
Heh heh

In three hours or four hours
We're talking about
Half the surgery

What's gonna happen?
You know what's gonna happen?
No

It's just ready
Don't worry
I'm gonna be here for a long time

Or it's tiredness
From the day
You died that day

You don't have a chance of spending the time
Since the night of the South Carolina

I really thought the night of the 7th

Must be sometime soon
If I had a time for my—

Evolutionary?
Well, if you believe—

You believe in mini-things
What would you like to do?

Until I get through, I'm gonna be in Washington

15

Would you still connect?

The hamburger from the pie
Afterward
Some chagrin

I'm not even saying
I'm suggesting

Ask me to say some things
Don't take away

Sleep for a while
You sleep for everybody

I notice it around here
Theater tickets

In several good ways
Another year

You sure?
You say, "Hunh?"

You imitate the language of your—
Or irritate it

Today means nothing
More than two

16

Who's this?
This can go back to the school board
Who's not paying a 13th?
Mr. What?
Syke's interest in this is ridiculous

17

My daughters never—
We need these bits
Bacon to cry
Andirons

It's only yesterday
Not much else today
She has one job
It's his job

This center feels so good
This year

Now you're a physician, right?
The essential journal is not the only journal
You know this—
I'm just thinking about—
Life for dinner is like hundreds of dollars
You have a hundred dollars in your savings bank
I want your own seat
Might find it also

18

The dominator doesn't tell me
You gotta leave a little secret

That ten cents gets devoted to

I'll do it if you want
Anybody anywhere else

Here we have the opposite on both sides
Yeah, we all talk like that
If we still talk
We started earlier to wonder
If you want to give us—

Raindrops on a puddly field

That's how people get there
Then I'll do a talk there
Just dash and talk

Joy, next time when you come home
They needed someone to write about China
They needed someone to write about sciences
Your year in the Caribbean, right?

19

I'm just not gonna vote for you
People!
It's been a shame so far

They don't care ... and they don't want you to come back
Don't say that

No VW used to do that
Around here

You can be his wife
God, it would be Israel

You asking me?
You roughed up...?

It's a truism

If you want
I can find you something else, too
Who? Like Mason? I don't know

The ice doesn't seem to be so ... tight

20

All this week
The theater
For flight

His own past
Perfume
Chocolate
Hamburgers are, too
Books have been changed
To football rooms

Do they share feathers?
Can't they afford to stay at home?
He passed it up
Because it depends on—me
He's going to take over from Jay, it looks to me

You would have to be dead to carry something ashore

21

Find out if he's there
A person to be reached
Hammerheads
Suppose he doesn't have it

You never rotted me
You were really nice to me, were you?

Running stars now
On a separate line

Which would save his life
Something else, wouldn't it?

Tonight's headline
Sanders
Manders tonight
Klondike Bill

Reilly's staying here
He says here about this thing
The danger is
I'm in a smart position but—
Comfortably situated
Stock action

See if you can smile
All that stuff
Cuz we wasn't there
Tama Maflani's in Denver

Dow's candy bars

Wait a minute
An hour or not
An hour or nothing
It would have to go by

She just does it
His youngest-youngest-youngest

Overshadowed by icky
By an icky layup
You should have stayed at football yesterday
So you didn't have to … differentiate

Deep-fingers Dan here did it two weeks ago
Whistleblowing

It sounds like several people
I don't just throw these out
No, you Northerners can
Well, the experience was longer
How was your visit

His only chance is to get some

You know which issues then?
Because we'll be free tonight
You know what I think
I think she likes you
We're not suited temperamentally
I'm so glad you remembered that

But let's dance an eleven o'clock movement every day
You wouldn't be well enough to pay for it

In quiet?
You keep saying that to yourself
Do you know when it opens again?
Yes, open the door in 90 minutes

Why do you spell maybe?
A little drairy
An angel in the cornfield

I'm not really eating anymore
I'm rested

Grab the milk
Grab the extra cheese
Why?
Because network isn't the answer here

I want to come down there, and calm them down
The city of Birmingham will have to wait
If so
If there is a yemma son
And if we don't have
If we lost some

Linky Smith describes how awful it is and becomes

I'm just an other
Soul sunk

We should have less racing

22

Tell me
Mountains

I wanted
Surety

The names up to me
He's running

Now I have to come with a program
Else I give you long distance

The constraints upon her
I knew Tracy doesn't expect anything

City Hall
Big-big-big fight to go into

Examples of nothing
Hurry up

Nastiness
And I've been thrown away

Her scream
Which is terrible

23

I bet you understand

She's leading us to pieces

24

Find on Tuesday night's place card

What did you do so new?

Down the road from the same fella
Some tent field

It really is something
You marry someone
You participate

It's so far gone

Your mirror

Not just hearing a whisper for each student

Niner did
Playmate

I want suspicion
I enjoy movies for their texture

This is the right size

Half Jewish
Gives to her

Getting off

A plate so far
CM   CM

Now we're in a state

Adler
He's gonna come back

25

You don't have to get attacked by one of these segments

The preferential treatment

Bar sales, including—
Power position in the city
Caught with his Rob Roy
I don't know why he wouldn't
He asks you what's in it
You don't know what it means

Icing on the soup

Say something
Just tell me

A sweet breeze
A white niece
In a traffic mansion
Holding on for dear life

OK
Okalay

76 singers
To eat?
She said me
That's so funny

We had those periods
They don't—carefully—sleep

The attorney general
Did Douglas?

They say it could be nice

That's right, you won't get a job
Cuz otherwise—

I'll try to
Let me do it, OK?
It really doesn't suit you

He might know a story
I know somebody who's going to—

It really is
Sounds terrible

I'm ready to move somewhere
Somewhere—exciting to—me
Cuz here
You can't do something
For me, anyway

I have my bell ring to listen to
My bell ring's a mess

She usually left her tickets there
She catered to you
You were just stuck
With this

I've been trying to take him to his cell and dorm room upstairs and
    see if he could take his basement

They're the last person to call

They might be trying to tell you, no matter what
For instance

Animals and music and all that

It's all right
It's a mineral matter

There's two batters

And a position

And pharmaceuticals

Clean out the study
Get me out of here

You reached back and started over

He's over 18 now
He doesn't need a TV
Or assistance

Disturbingly
So that's good

This isn't the curious lady
This is the difficult one

You seem too upset
You certainly-certainly do

Our money is so obsessive—
Such human

It wasn't such a great system
It was all fiction

He's like on another line right now

Chris, care to be the star?

And have to put on double uniforms

It ain't easy
To use another management

Yo
You want to stay on top
I see what you want to do now

Of the single East, I'll send you
If you don't want—

No, it's not black
It's not a lethal guard
It can't be

What kind of work?
A spot on August 19

She's gonna come back again
She comes on Sunday

Three
Four
One

Bobby Assistant
Baby Tillis

A positive
For us
Sighting him

New York

Available for six thirty

You know, Bo, speak up

There's nothing wrong with him now
Today united
Nothing wrong with him now?

Feet up the basement—floor

So is Andy

A little bit
I chase him for once
You got the answer

Less pita bowl
Three dozen sklat?

Overtime on me
On his thesis
To tell me

26

He had the sun

See, it's a faint breath

Swallow
Words [worlds?] swallow

And stay away from hating beans

Richard snared his foot
Purposefully
On his desk
You seemed to miss it

So this is
Wayne's establishing it!

Meg and I are gonna talk this evening, bro

The time you're still in school
Did you have a fancy house?

But do me a favor

The grocery store
River in Pluto

Like something with his Vexican or something

You're in the city already in Brooklyn
City?
It really is
I think it's worth it
I love the city

✳

West of horse country
The contrast
Is your Quaker on the same kind of lunch

Oh
We see
I see
But we'll see if we can

Everyone
Eyes wide open

Road-running
To everybody else

Respects a lot of his terms

The possibilities seepy
Consolidation sucks

My friend Anne lives in Trenton now
The choice is in Manhattan

They're older folks, too
They're gonna return the same story

Veiled in circumstance, will ya?

I don't!
I used to be so smart

You botch—yourself up
Since I put my shoes on, ya hear me?

That's what I'm gonna start doing more than then

Please let me know
They stink in small
I couldn't care less if they care not

Forty semantics lessons
Waiting for me

27

You know, it's usually nonsense
Proust is better

St. Louis

They may pig 'em

You know the difference

Eddy
Ostinsky
Hector

The trombone, try it

What I'm saying

You don't understand me
I unnerstan you, son

You may stay sober

It's ticketed
In reverse

The spire booth
Rich to the last ounce

Skelly, Ghelly, Ghelly
He goes on to say

There, it did again, you—

Which is done
You can see today

In Steve's, can you get me—

Maybe, just maybe
Mybe

Kaiser's best friend
Who's attempting to do that?

Both can handle six inches

Arlen's miserable
It doesn't sound like I can see 'im

Seven years ago is—already—three years ago

The beauty box is a double—
It's a bubbler

Deena
Deena, Deena

That's pretty good, right?
Phoenix schools are gonna take a look at this?
Tantamount—to your credit
The assignment's in it
Later

The speedometer
Welcome back

And because he's starving, eats their food
Eats their food cuz of that?
Mandatory eating habits, as you do

Cokey
Maybe Sunday
It's the other way around

I used to say that
Yes, I did

It's a kind of seasons, too—see this?
There's something going on there

Wednesday morning, as early in the morning

They're getting more intensely
So it's not as if—justice is on your side

Cuz he finished his staw-ree
But it seems to be telling you the other thing
Inside the game yesterday

Prospect Park is a beautiful—
Yes, it is

What's going on at Pound's place?
His place is great

Could you put a stop on this?
As long as you tell me about crawling

I guess they really do work

Spinning round
Syrup

The twins deserve it
But he's ten foot—

Of all things
Of all things
By the way, Emily thinks it's OK
Do you?

Just run to your phone for once
And two meatballs after all

Just three
So they don't get crowded anymore
No shower tonight

Fish oil I don't have to judge

Your calendar wife's thing
Is this it?

At first, if it's impossible
To stop a triangle

28

At least through many areas

Confusion reigns
It really does

Alright for him
Because she was much better

For total control
It's not Christmas's camp

Go ahead
Today's—
Today's the first—

Your soulful—
No, I came outside of your door

The hair is the oldest
The hairdressing room is the best

And sits there like a rebel to you
You, you're the most

Whose tabors are there?
You haven't even started

When I open these doors, I can't tell if it's Alice Quinn's voice or
someone else

All such thoughts are such a bore
Only interesting for what they provoke

29

Honesty, Mike
They always make a point of giving you something

The Academy Award
Good looking
A movie, didn't I tell you?

Vaporized
And you're gonna drive—right out of—the dream room

It's all there
They buried it!?

A college, I find

In the discos and not
High school, you're going to the disco

One guy took an 8:30, 8:30 train

I did, on my bonus to you

Out of my system
Out of—my—sys-tum

Foundation football
On top of the all-star game

He's a decent player
We're still gonna git—
The bot scenery

The clinical stat from side to side
This was one of his most—doop!

W Poison Ivy FM
That is so dumb

The end of the night

They measured it
Thank you very much

Sitting down on the sidewalk

We'd go on the Hill
It's gonna fish out

Did you see the voicemail
Who would have had to kill him?

The more he yelled at you

They're all drivel
They're all liberal

Get under the wires of the thing

Go to the same place twice
Well, you can go to Baltimore

I've been out swimming
I've been around here
Can I *get* my clothes!

Later
You *did* everything!

We figured it out
We just didn't want to—hold us

On the Internet
The Internet has the perfect line for you
Have you ever written—

For the dinner
And they're in the pretty bank already

You want to see it, some other pictures
Another picture

Go for it
All, dude

Go in the right directions
Work for records
The kids are a group

30

They just want to let you know

He did a fine job?
Why?
Weren't there millions of reasons?

I can't believe you
For the national championship

Put an Elvis rerun
What?

After Giuliani
Double vision

Like mine
Could he fire you?
He says yes

Termajeration
It abutted me one

You're gonna go in and meet this gal

Are you a big talker? Talker?

His consciousness is an advance
Michael, would you?

It won't be a championship either

Cake
Maybe they get my cake—and my day!

Michael, you should have heard—

I sleep

I sleep

We're not gonna do that

I don't have any anticipation
I don't have to listen to any other analyst either

The rock 'em plate

Not just—wishy-washy
Washy-washy

Ponds e-mail

Average ability
Robberability
Robberability

For some people
By one group

Short openings
Do you want flour?

The most soporific thing imaginable

They are now gone
They always have a *way* of doing it
Sometimes from a strategy

Hey, temproid
Sometimes the slowness is unbearable

You can snort a bit more
You can stop it

That's not nice
Alright
You begin to gobble, too

In the government's campaign

Resplendent

The intermission
I don't think in terms of—

I like Beatrice
Are you going to intellectualize it?

The meaning of his work is totally obscure

With nothing else to do
Wherever I am—very upset
But I got on a Conair flight, near midnight

Your brother wants to be your servant

Hours to get it started
Would you stop now?

This one is from the year of the All-American baby carriage
But they were in them
The way they put away babies was the best protocol
No, this was

Rip a cold
Now do that again

He had a reason now

You have to title me
Title me!

You get to a point where the deformations are too strong

This is Nicholas News
He wrote it this afternoon

A red layer
Two hours over on me

Going through the castle was so small

31

He doesn't hear any more voices

Jane was there
What?
In the nume

You're excused to make false calls, choices
Amusing
Anymore

A hundred
Lesson

First, you help
Very senior people
A lot of fun
Air the case
Please, do not work on it

…doesn't care about anything
The less you know
…cares

Master of Easter
Stephen Wyndham

You sick?
They're gonna build a new 3rd Street

32

Quote

Humungous
Right the trampo

Now you don't know anybody
You gonna take me off the list?

Uh
One city
Would you?

A whole son are resigning

What?

Two nice little notes

…small things
I'll tell you what, my—

But this is what—

…associates
I guess so

Rogers

Let's leave it there
Just leave it there

33

We'll have to decide
We'll *see*

Pictures
It's all the same
You've seen me—

The Times wrote an article

For force
Most of it

Phenomenally well
Thank you

I take sweets over to the meat [meet?]

In those eyes-ez
So instead

Cuz they don't care less

We're there
All good things

The track is on us
On 'em
It hits a word

Standing around
Wednesday
You mean it

My girl is at school now
My goodness gracious
Have I just spent subway

It's such a nasty thing
It's so funny it gave such scares to—

Oh, Natalie lets us all play

You know, I can't get to it and knock down

A headline is special
Is the whole time special?

I don't think we can talk about this anymore
That's news for us

Boop Anne on the nose

I have a battlefield
I have some brothers
Look it up, the southern carosofel

Closed me and her two countries
Zero
Remember, the whole country knows it
And they're going to answer specially for it
Of course, you know where it's at, too
What it means to be American
Putting America through the high-tech motions

34

Marshall Coleman

Do you recall a journal?

The Winter Garden
So busy

Meridian

Plum brandy

Now it's time to take us off
You begin to get involved with—

Who knows?
To soften the blow—

Just because she said she would

It was still crowded
It was really, really nice

You were missing Flight—
Not by minutes, by 24 hours

I still don't know

Donald Grant Incorporated

Jackal's the task
And then she didn't—

A guideline in thinking now
Because hers is so terrifying
She also gave us some books

35

This is not a sleepy one
It's not a sleepy one

I just want to miss you

Exackly

Yeah
The girl might not

You know
Wait till Friday night

Grandma hasn't spoken for years

A lot of that is related to the housing market

Oh no
No question about what I'm doing
I have no idea

I don't even want to talk to him
Er, alright?

Narwhal, listen

Keep it fenced
Keep it fenced

...tells us periods of time you can—

On either side of the canyon

Nothing eats ya up like landlords

6.5?

For it to be fashionable

They gave her a building store
Isn't that terrible?

Outside of his hornets

Return it to himself

You tried to get in?

In your head, you're reading Emmeridge
In your head, you're reading Emmeridge

The whole thing sounds so stupid
Same to giggle

The essence of you, as far as I'm concerned

Then leave him out
Keep him before he comes out

Look, Andre has the documentary

What's he doing after the salary changes?
You lock up employees—

The savings don't amount to so much

You see, that's what I'm saying

So sure enough—
He turned it up

He's one of the worst people I've ever known

He saw this bit coming

I don't expect to make a service

Very difficult times

Very difficult times
Very difficult times

"It's not for me to say" [Johnny Mathis singing in a TV commercial]
I don't favor that

Yes, it is

36

Paul sometimes
What was him?
The family—
What a jerk
They all play the same
They speak like I do

Life in prison
You said that a month ago

America's a movie playing on many channels

You seem like a fairly mixed-up—

It just depresses me
You depress me

37

Harassment
Some favorite signs
Charlie knew that bed
Turn on "The Doors"
On some level

He was a great ... player
$150 million a year

They should be the same
There's a lot of things you have to do
You're on your second cup of coffee
Listen to this thing work

It's a painkiller
It doesn't kill ya'

I should be blunt
Waymus stapyu horn
It's this one, right here
I first wrote them down
In the mack church

You say it's OK
Us OK

In other words
You would do that

Really?
Because if it's becoming a—

Kenny ought to know

     ✳

They don't want to be hurting you
…is not to live with the answers

The joy of
What do you mean?

You got to be defensive, Harry
Opens your eyes, like listen to this Ouija

*

They were gonna—make a law mistake
Thad Green
What, uh, you up in your sight?

They thought—you know
Today's
Ninety days

Let's see what next year's like
But you might want to quit

We're almost ready to give full-time
Be ready full-time

Physically, it's not impossible—to move with less economy
Changes in the structure
You want to move 'em and oversee them and—

This is a logical
An office
A logical impact on it

It was a pain in the neck
Ocean stand

I told you
She's getting married
I told you I got stuff to do

He doesn't know when it's gonna happen, but it's soon

38

It will always keep its place

You to Pennsylvania

Is he not nice to you—or do you care?
He has been so—

I might side along with him
Asshole!

I'm saving
What am I saving for?

They grew walls, period
That's why we're gonna walk away

Despite faith in lows [lulls?], this work is coming out

He could either take his horses in for a physical
Or his voice out of his stomach

Of course you have

He saw that's my coat
He says, "It's mine"

You'll have some cash in your hand

You feel something happen
You use it, of course
You used it short time, they used it long time

It's as easy as choking on something
As anything you want

I'm doing my poorest
Equally poor

39

It's another thing
It doesn't
It was—nice

Big deal costs little typical money
Typical money, typical money

When he comes

Across the river, it's being done by a Baptist
Whom society really seems to help

The husband just doesn't like anything
On a study of one

I have not seen you on Tuesday nights

Just before parents are taken next weekend

That's just a side of things
Well, he's uh here

Cassandra
It's just never going to go anywhere

Did you show him how to do it?
Did he master the shovel?
Also using the fish

What day is it?
Eat 'em up, eat 'em up, eat 'em up

Never smoking
How 'm I gonna change the world?
How 'm I gonna get anywhere?

40

You don't mind if I lose this weight?

In the summer sometimes
He cooked

The main [Maine?] office
It's really just us
Because his character

Is that his name?
At the Navy Yard

…oases for me
How many for guests?

Tables or chairs
As you know, six years
You need six years

I just don't think about it
Let's work it out

*

It's basically acceptable and we should use it
There was the 5 ¼
There was the 6 ½

*

So why didn't you stop thinking about me?
And stop being so hungry

…go between the lines and read it
That's a nice poisonous one

People didn't like that stuff

Why?

If I picked it up in 10 minutes

They're not tight, Daddy
They're tight, Charlotte, I know they are
You're gonna get a sense how tight this is
This is that rock fitting into place

You think it was smarter?
Yes
And cheaper?
Yes

It would never take longer

So big and bad here

I've played other games with you

He has much better deals than you think

Have a seat
You have that for an instant

Shows on the air
We're dead

So sad in the ego tonight
You see each person running out of their background

Did you eat anything since 1
No

The state of their minds buried

41

You see what you're doing?
Three times a week
When it's good for her—

I'm working on a
I'm working on a
I'm working on the questions

So OK, don't do it
Do it, don't do it

42

...of fate [state?] last night

It had all those provisions

Improvident nightfalls

And save up on a CD recorder

We want to exhaust the possibilities

Just like he's off of

Only small amounts of it

...is languishing, is uncalled for

Free has it for a million
We haven't seen the presidential library

Pathetic!

Then it was the NFL passing
For girls—

They took off kindergarten

Snyder
Snyder
Snyder
Snyder
After that
Nine months

Absolutely
Which I think I will
And I won't

Surely wanted to be a backstroker

Get 'em cheerful
Earful

Get his hands on it
Pretty soon, that's what he wants to do

Nasty common ground
So what you're missing—is—this recording

If it doesn't, he was just ignoring altered states of being

Get the hunger pieces on the air
Let's do that

I'm not asking where this is going to go

My student went right to Shearson
Stick around for George Pierson

It looks more stuffy in here

High basketball seasons
To be associated with this

Who thought he was going to be tough?
Is that who the lawyer thought he would be?

But widening the colors

They were getting serious up there
Are some of these people in their—

43

Fuck off!
The bastard

Trailing swans
Horrible as it may sound

Do it the way he knows
He does a job
He once [won't?] assume

I didn't play any tennis for you
Don't tell anybody

Miss lends a tip
He's left the firm
They said ABC

Are we here?

44

How ya doin'?
How ya doin'?
And how ya doin'?

...tapes themselves

Do you know what type of work she has?
Did you look at her?

The attacker's a big bunch
There's stuff that's—
Too radical as it is

They both have got something to say

45

This one
The position was a nice one

…hails from there

The yellow tag, and you can use three words

And I think retrospectively
We can turn our cheeks again

46

You don't know where help will come from

Yup
It gave me a beautiful uh

Who was Jody?
Cuz I never did see him again

His beams have been tossed
Because he'd gone into this

From a few years ago
Free school

Vaguely manage to communicate

You have to train your sweater
Before you—
You got no boots

In the school system
You know, they're sold

Murky people
Thank the people who work for him
Nice to hear about him

Some days I'm not up to doing much
You know who I am?

That's their second
That's their second window

Life was wrong
I was with you this morning, telling you about it

47

They come in all shapes and sizes
Please don't do that now

The school's no longer educating the kids
Aren't they?
I don't know

We're only drivers

To the Tylenol

Really adds a little, too
Do you know anything?

On the first day percentagewise
...so it was an interesting conversation

And a voice got up there and started—
—Still standing there

You've got to know
You're supposed to know

A cellphone so I can see what's happening

48

Look at that
Look at that
Look at that

He done a thousand
He done zillions

This is a hard time to ask questions
And that's the answer

I remember, but I used to think
You remember, but you used to get angry

Yeah sure
Would you like to?
Yeah sure

And offer to me when it's gonna come to Moody?

The only thing I'm mad about is … Interview

Tina
DZ I'm negotiating

Math, do municipally
Math, do miserably?

49

Take you somewhere else
Now, to step over them

Oh God, I shouldn't have been so pleasant
The West Bank is more interesting

Tulips, however

On the pleasure
On the history
On the eleventh

I guess so

No, he's not the thinnest
Not thinnest

It may not be advisable

Can you get a license for that

And I was

...developing in southeastern France
And their neighbors—

It may make the two parts more—
—They certainly don't

Once you're there, of course, it's been there

Peterson
A uniform position
Peterson's in

Whatever you want is fine with me
If you want presents, as I said

No matches on Sunday night
On Nissan

Cuz everyone's new

The house sleeps all night

Lynch knows it's his, not Peter's

...any historical sites anymore
By $50,000

Who works on it
So don't work on it

...gives a better clue
And it comes from the secret

50

They're the biggest eyelashes in your life

Last night
Just last night

Now it's going forward
Get up and set the gears

You must be doing something wrong
The minute the upheavals

Skip it

When you're watching one person

Sorrow classes
They're tomorrow

If you get closed up
Who's the next one who's gonna do it

By the time I noticed
Now my wife doesn't even notice

No more cigarettes
That would be momentous
Imagine that

But you have to keep on

To let music in and everything
Or leave us alone

Statue
…on probation

You know it sounds funny—

Singing
I think it was physical
Not many minutes, I know that
I was thinking of doing something for you
Like the Winter Garden

They were going to appear in order
The 25th of January

But I found a different place

Which is, of course
Which is, of course, record labels

I didn't know that
I thought we were friends with everybody

Everyone claims—
And they have no desire to desert themselves

However, that will end
Airplane aneurysms, which aren't ours, huh

Plenty of clothes, for the obvious reasons

Such luck as we entrust the almighty

And I told you no
Of any size
But I'm not gonna do anything

And then, there's all the communication

Got a bit of law on our hands

Along a different—
A juvenile delinquency

We need a tillion civilians
I want you to take over their hardware store

You know what he said really loud
Can I tell you what this makes me feel like

One a vacation
From the family of friends
A mistake

How do you know all this
How do you know this

51

You're faded [fated?] already

Get relatives in for free

Intercom
Become an interviewer?

I want to go back
A very slight interaction
But if you come back here

The problem
I don't think there's going to be enough

So a long time ago
He couldn't do it

The article was originally written
With—her support

Between my father and—
My father, you know—

Write down the verbs
Clarence Munson

I don't care
Maybe I'm not fooling around enough right there for anybody

She's in the left wing
We went over that

You wanna take a look, Mike
Yes, I'd like to

First look at it
We're gonna throw a football

Jerry Atkins & Co.

Three really are frozen

Brunswick, you know, I mean

And they're gonna win, right?
I don't know exactly what I want to do

It's a very selective way of praying
It's all—
I mean—

Real step-walking upon others

Do anything now?
Get your number and do nothing now?

All of you are gonna know more about French all of a sudden
I think that's probably been around the whole time

Window, too
There, our whole door locked

52

Have a 7:15

No risk again

You're not going off to pay for it

And there were more golden girls near Broadway

But then that'll require some ideas

…and there'll be a legal answer
Richard'll have some with me

The joy and … the listening and the product of listening

We don't go to the top anymore

At Red Vine
Didn't you see her?
We saw a lot of him

Every step of the way
I'll come back

A bunch is cold
Icy cold, let me taste it

You get a lot of parents

53

Be quiet
I hear them

Not mapped out
What is it—

When a guy
At the moment

California
The strong strong strong
They're gonna hold ya up

Around vaguely
No star

Right of you to run
You have to ask yourself
Would you notice?

Is he going to leave the household as short as he leaves the palace?

I'll have to bring it back
But you don't really listen

Especially in his canna
You know he nearly has a—

There's some hotel in you

Look for your taunted
Don't ya stand it

Now there is a girl
Collection of—

I don't know who these people today are

Don't get mad about it
Don't get mad about it

Who would say that?

A confidence—
Not with any preference in any place

Slow everything up

We're not really doing much right now
In another world

As sight
It ain't so easy

Tulsa also made the strong impression
With Isabel

54

Your illustrious ones
Your glorious ones

And you can't get everybody
No, you can't get anybody

...is American
Up and down

Now it's the dark waters
That you like waters

Done right when you shouldn't
One second

You know, this one is the best
To know this one

A record
Of what there was to learn

And went there 20 hours a day
And she got away with it

55

The distance effects

Why didn't they go see—
Yesterday
Yesterday what?

He's coming back to Vermont
He had your keys

You've got to know that
Minor transitions as bodies

56

In the Calanida
North Pole

She wrote it down

What stands out for me

Pick a place
Get some motors

At least we have a place that's alright
We don't need any services
That's something we didn't do

He resented that
The working Sunday

He telephoned
Frank excuses

B's the only one
Who's following up with any regularity

We may not have done as much as we could
We did more

People can't afford it
We're gonna—for you
For you
For you

Then the punta de vista has left

There's another sponge
A segment

Why's the storm on?

The Eskimos can come up
And fry the door

Night's the snow moth
Got your snow moth

They shoot the wings head off

She can't do it tonight
Oh yick

I've been tryin' for a long time
Take the works out
Keep the works out
The orange chick

It was stunning
It wasn't stunning, was it?
Snow

…they say that's it
I'm sorry

I'll just go upstairs and catch up
Maybe if you have some

She wanted the child to be in school
In school every day
And asleep every night

57

As soon as people stop mattering to each other

The best way to do it
Finger the upholstery

Early morning
No one knew

One catastrophe
One sylvan

Now if I'd settled again
I might start paying myself

An almost ultimate part of the soul
On a healing basis

Snows, you know
The whole has to get siding

The Russian youth movement

It's random good
A mashiki

You in enough trouble

Few books make much difference
The class of any existence

We ain't falling in the woods anymore
Rattling any chains

When you get in a scoff
With everything

It was from Diglia

58

You'll see something yourself in a few minutes

Tonight, if I need you most

He's changed my mind a lot

59

You can stand to give glory a little bit

You get money in the front seat if you don't give in
It was Daniel, Daniel, Daniel
The Davis Foundation

Why are we not doing other things?
And where are we not doing other things?

We're seeing Jimmy Palmer
The top seed in the tennis, stand right there
And stand right here

You say your name is Len
You ought to say who it is

Right in front of the church is Dan
Yeah, you better do that now
You better talk to May
One four ha ha ha

It's too bad we lose these kids already
But this does take some time before you can fix it

The ships were not too late for us this year
It knew where to go as soon as it landed
Nova Scotia

Mom learned how to stay free
And do the first thin jobs

60

Let us now go back to sleep and never wake up

Nearest to what you wanted
Nor the socially accepted

...requires the meditation

Dick Town used to play this?

Don't be silly
It's a stupid idea

61

You don't have any cans or something?

You run out of room for solid ground
She's gonna appreciate that

Washed and heavy
I want to take advantage of this

Flabby, patronizing

You know what I said to Hamilton?
No

We're in a book to keep the chaos done

A yawning
Number five

I have my own chair on the bush, Daddy

The company's well
You know, you owe me—

Charlotte feels like taking a nap

Yesterday I ironed out an argument with Stephen
Just around the corner tomorrow

Queer cat didn't even know it

62

If I tell ya on the week

…could walk in on the old man

You're supposed to get anything

Well, she had flowers against her mother

The main Roosevelt appointed the house in white

I wouldn't have tried to do that

I needed something

I was beside my mama for a warm second

She is lost to us both

And the big surprise

63

I don't really want to think about him at this point in my life

I like the aeration
Then the breeze comes

Then he could be right there

You feel pulled down
To Pittsburgh

It's been very stable this year
I didn't want to say anything

Will I need to take you all?
I'm not sure what Dave said

Today was this day I had to write
You're right

We still have the hairy guy in
Last night and the—

We just got in
We just got in
It didn't
How did you do that?

…is not getting napped
Not even right now

They're coming
They're coming
The main spur for finding out

We didn't have to fear the hurdling

Before that, gases in Pennsylvania
You couldn't—the skin

64

It's ghastly original
The kids would like to do something

We're gonna use them

I asked you about it
With full disclosure and due diligence

Why would we want to see this
When did you see me

When Crystal owned the place
I can't see the city, I can't see the city

Take this home so you can't do that
It was like cancer

He can't get out there
And he doesn't now

It turns out his school has no values of its own
Yeah, we don't have enough time at the beach

65

Why don't you take it away from them?

The pull-ups stank

You don't have visitors
You know how to do it
You know how to do it, do you?

How you feeling now?
A lot of it has to do with—

As a friend
"No one loves me as much as you love me" [a man singing]

He's there, by definition
Just as misty
At home

What's the size of this brick
What's the size of this brick
You're counting when I call meetings

Watch out for that ringleader
Don't let her touch that ringleader!

This is a scene in a bank account
A history of affairs
I don't know!

Get the 3-year-old in pajamas
Put it in your arms and see why it looks so good

Cuz you said 3 o'clock
3 o'clock
4 o'clock

Go ahead
Go to bed now
If you're gonna go to sleep

66

We will hear things
Soon enough

Just being able
And insulting

But it's short, sweet

Detail me on that one

Assist on
They weren't happy with it

How should David

Grew conservative
To themselves
Their money

It's not necessary to hurt my neck
Hurt myself

They passed me
You afterward made your shorts hour

Foisted on me for some stallions
And when I signed up, I didn't sign for—

The pay is good

The same day—the sneakers are here

…which tells me you—
…so much

Glisses
I-can't-stand-to-be-Miss America

The only wording for the scouts is

...navigate those children, ever
Ever listen to Roberta's story

His line of career
His whole antisocial

Can you help me just a little
One—

You linked with another motor trend

Set in the cave in Africa
The confines of—

We didn't get it
We didn't want this year as a ... calmer

The cow cars
Hallelujah

Brand-new players
I thought you said a new pants set

This is my horizon
And end zone

Open your eyes
Open your mouth in a special way

His idea
Once

Who could incite your infatuation?

You true to you, baby
You You You

A floodwatch
...antenna

67

We will not know now

And what about the leveled town
Leveled by hurricane
The bright yellow town
The bright yellow sun

At the end of the day
Still hot

No one really knows

I don't have a hard time getting the car signed
Just upon sharing

What about Cody?
He suited you

On the express
The cow didn't bite
Nobody did smell the cattle

They gave a triangular
Her opinion

I'm gonna give it to them

Sorry
You see-ee-ee, boys

I want you to join in, to rest the night with us
Cuz then, it's not too much

What steef is that?

On the floor of the closet
In the sea house and all

Glad you asked that
We're just dumb

They'd find a place called heaven

By subjugations

As we went through the whole system
And we made the plans

Of students
Students who have never been—
...for real

I loathed my
I loathed my
I loathed my
Oh, citizenship

...why nobody's here

In the It-ly
One reason you shouldn't—

68

She passes over a pessian
As the colonel would say

The accurate dither
You want one of Pino's

Under intensified discussion of the jazz ensemble
Of course, it was a lucky life and stuff

And then he turned
I you flagellate

Wore it up
C'mon, you dog
You might miss yourself in my arms

What's valuable to people many times

Anonymity
After stormy weather

Very expensive

Even if it's a function that's been working?

Our daughter is too loud for your kids and their case
Because they sing each other

My mom's thousands
I'm gonna try livin' off her

It doesn't make it big
The window's blackout

People believe it

That's the second part

That's the second part of the drug—
…they're going into
If the second is my father

I'm trying to say
I'm saying

That payment for a loan he made that night

69

Abraham, go home
The Peshmerga

You started
We started

You don't just kiss items

These are almost—
Free fold

That's what Stevens again

The Jupiter flight
The world is a city below the clouds, below the mountains

I want you to—
Stay the nurse

I shake my head at that

> *

It is, I believe, time for me for what?

He was outside on his own different contract
He didn't get in there

We could in Daverton
It took us out of our way

Considering how everything is
It should truly be another day in school

It's just too much for her
The cliffs
She can't go back up anymore

70

It's all going to—
Consumers

Casual at 20
20 is enough

It would be—
Bag-in licenses
He might be ready

Down the way, I didn't want to grasp it, you know, last week

It gives him peanuts and—
…and low, and discarded

The very problem with that is this little mechanical engineer we have
A maniacal experiment

The Egyptians had to eat western Mexicans
…a little bit
That's the only place I could go

Michael, then, have a seat
You are too small
You wanted to say that… the most
It's not easy to do that
You have to either invent or—
You have a need of an overseas, supersonic

Is this a feeding on the tired spirit?
A replenishing?

MICHAEL HANDLER RUBY is the author of five poetry books: *At an Intersection* (Alef Books, 2002), *Window on the City* (BlazeVOX [books], 2006), *The Edge of the Underworld* (BlazeVOX, 2010), *Compulsive Words* (BlazeVOX, 2010) and *The Star-Spangled Banner* (Dusie, 2011). A sixth poetry book, *American Songbook*, is forthcoming from Ugly Duckling Presse. He is also the editor of *Washtenaw County Jail and Other Writings* by David Herfort (Xlibris, 2005). A graduate of Harvard College and Brown University's writing program, he lives in Brooklyn and works as an editor of U.S. news and political articles at *The Wall Street Journal*.

CPSIA information can be obtained at www.ICGtesting.com
Printed in the USA
BVOW080941300413

319426BV00001B/26/P